THE MARKETING CENTURY

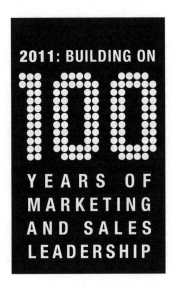

2011: BUILDING ON 100 YEARS OF MARKETING AND SALES LEADERSHIP

2011

A century
of building
professional
status and
recognition

cim.co.uk/100

THE MARKETING CENTURY

HOW MARKETING DRIVES BUSINESS

AND SHAPES SOCIETY

THE CHARTERED INSTITUTE OF MARKETING

EDITED BY JEREMY KOURDI

A John Wiley & Sons, Ltd., Publication

ISBN 978-0-470-66015-7 (hardback), ISBN 978-1-119-99359-9 (ebk),
ISBN 978-1-119-97413-0 (ebk), ISBN 978-1-119-97414-7 (ebk)

A catalogue record for this book is available from the British Library.

Typeset in 10/14.5 pt FF Scala by Toppan Best-set Premedia Limited, Hong Kong
Printed in Great Britain by TJ International Ltd, Padstow, Cornwall, UK

CONTENTS

INTRODUCTION TO THE MARKETING CENTURY

Rod Wilkes, Chief Executive, the Chartered Institute of Marketing

Rod Wilkes is Chief Executive of The Chartered Institute of Marketing, the leading international professional marketing body with approximately 50,000 members worldwide.

The Chartered Institute of Marketing (CIM) is unique in its ability to give marketing professionals a place to learn, develop and belong. In this introduction Rod Wilkes, the Institute's Chief Executive, explains about the marketing century, the development of the Institute and how marketing drives business and shapes society.

One hundred years of marketing

The development of the Institute, since it was established in 1911, closely reflects the growth and progress of business in general and marketing in particular. Just as marketing has developed as an activity that is highly valued, varied and vital in its contribution to business success, so the Institute's work has expanded as an indispensable source of insight, guidance and practical support.

> Marketing is a philosophy – *everyone* in an organisation must be a marketer. Above all, a clear focus on customers and markets is vital and the whole board needs to understand marketing.

This book, written to celebrate the Institute's centenary, explains how the key elements of marketing have developed, how the various aspects of marketing contribute to performance, what it is that great marketers do and how the discipline of marketing may develop in the future. The dynamics and key trends in marketing are clearly described, as well as best practice. While *The Marketing Century* aptly describes the 100 years since 1911, it also describes the twenty-first century: a time when possessing the ability to understand and connect with customers is more rewarding, complex and valuable than ever.

The origins and development of the Institute

The Chartered Institute of Marketing was established in 1911 and incorporated by Royal Charter in 1989. Originally named the Sales Managers' Association, it arrived at a time when the science and art of management was in its infancy. The evolution of the Institute shows a history of helping marketing professionals to learn about the discipline, develop their skills and belong to a wider community.

In 1921 the Sales Manager's Association became the Incorporated Sales Manager's Association (ISMA) and the Institute's origins and name highlight another point of lasting significance: the fact that marketing also includes *sales* as a related activity in the same discipline. The growth and development of the Institute continued in the 1920s, with the library being formed in 1923 and the first certificate examinations delivered in 1928. The Institute continued to grow and it was during the Second World War that correspondence courses in sales management were first introduced. In 1952, His Royal Highness, The Prince Philip, Duke of Edinburgh, became the organisation's patron, and in 1955 the Institute became a founder member of the European Contact Group of Sales and Marketing Associations, later to become the EMC. This tendency to work in a collegiate way with other organisations to promote marketing remains an important characteristic of the Institute.

The ISMA became the Institute of Marketing and Sales Management in 1960, and a year later the Diploma in Marketing was introduced. In 1968 the organisation changed its name again, becoming the Institute of Marketing. The Institute purchased its present home at Moor Hall in Cookham in 1971. This site has become firmly established as the head office and the Institute's centre for training and development.

> More people than ever before are now engaged in marketing and its significance and potential impact have never been greater. Because of this, it is immensely valuable to have an institution, awards and qualifications that are rigorous, relevant and universally respected.

Another significant milestone in the development of professional marketing was achieved in 1975 when the Institute launched the Marketing Code of Practice. This highlighted the growing recognition during the 1970s and 1980s of professional marketing as an essential aspect of business. This was followed in 1989 by the award of the Institute's Royal Charter, becoming the Chartered Institute of Marketing. Continuing Professional Development (CPD) – a vital and enduring aspect of professional marketing – was formally established in 1993, with the first Chartered Marketers receiving their awards in 1998.

A twenty-first-century Institute

The CIM's purpose

Throughout its history, the Institute's priority has been to support the development of professional marketing and marketers. This purpose has achieved renewed vigour in the twenty-first century, a time that can be fairly described as the marketing century. Now, more than ever, the Institute's purpose is to be at the heart of marketing by giving the profession a place to learn, develop and belong. This has several practical elements.

Education and learning

The Institute provides formal learning through two channels: first, by directly delivering training and awards in marketing and sales; second, by delivering the highest-quality practice-based awards through a network of study centres in the UK and internationally. In particular, the Institute is one of the world's leading providers of marketing qualifications, training courses and tailored training.

The CIM's marketing and sales qualifications are taught by some of the best minds in global marketing. They are informed by what is happening in the industry, so they are relevant for twenty-first-century marketers at all levels of their career. As a result, they are widely recognised by UK employers as being the premier marketing qualifications.

The Institute's purpose to provide world-class education and learning also means that it delivers more than 120 marketing, sales and business courses, ranging from digital marketing to brand management. These are continually evolving to meet the needs of marketing executives at all levels – from beginner to the boardroom. The Institute's courses are also rigorous and practical, enabling

> The Institute is one of the world's leading providers of marketing qualifications, training courses and tailored training.

executives to develop the latest skills and thinking. As well as delivering public or 'open' programmes, the Institute also tailors its qualifications and training courses to meet each organisation's needs. Given that one of the major trends in marketing over recent years has been towards greater customisation and flexibility and a clear understanding of customers' needs, it is entirely appropriate that the Institute should reflect this in the services it offers.

One fact that is clearly evident from reading this book is the extent to which the last 100 years have seen a rapid rise in the number of enterprises, markets, products and contexts in which an increasing number of individuals are participating in 'marketing'. It is an activity that has grown in scope, impact, significance and application. More people than ever before are now engaged in the fast-changing world of marketing and its significance and potential impact have never been greater. Because of this, it is immensely valuable to have an institution, awards and qualifications that are rigorous, relevant and universally respected.

Developing

The Institute strives to be the first point of call for marketing information, knowledge and insight. Its role is to develop the profession in general and practitioners in particular, and this is achieved in several ways. The first is by promoting Continuing Professional Development (CPD) as an essential personal and professional responsibility. The Institute's development role is also fulfilled by engaging with government and other key groups so that marketing continues to be recognised as an essential business discipline. The Institute also develops the profession and practitioners by providing best-practice guidance and content to the marketing and business community and, finally, by delivering information and insight regarding current and future marketing issues.

This reflects the pace of the change taking place in marketing and the need for professionals to develop their skills continuously and engage in lifelong learning.

It is entirely appropriate that a profession that relies on action, observation and improvement, as well as personalisation, should value lifelong learning and development. Just as the best businesses seek to understand and develop in a way that keeps them connected with their customers and the communities they serve, so great marketers also develop their skills and ability to compete and serve customers.

This book highlights why this aspect of the Institute's work is so significant. The worlds of public relations, sustainable marketing, advertising, branding and digital marketing, to name only a few, have changed dramatically in not much more than a decade or two. While some perennial issues endure through the ages and across marketing disciplines (such as the need to learn, develop and belong), there are many other issues that are changing continually, even *daily*. Given this unparalleled and accelerating pace of change, the Institute's role in helping people at all levels to improve their understanding of these changing expectations, challenges and opportunities is vital.

Belonging

The Chartered Institute of Marketing strives to be at the heart of marketing communities. This is achieved by facilitating the largest community of marketing professionals in the world, by developing a range of communities that enable the Institute to engage with marketers on several different levels and by promoting the benefits of professional membership.

Again, it seems entirely appropriate that a discipline that strives to connect with people on an individual level and with those from a diverse array of cultures and contexts should be concerned with community. This links closely with the need to learn and belong and it recognises that, as well as being a rigorous, data-driven activity, marketing also has a human, social and personal character. It is both science and art.

The result

The dynamic, thriving nature of marketing is highlighted by several facts about the Institute. For example, professional membership continues to increase in the UK and internationally (in 2009, international membership rose by 7 per cent). The Institute supports approximately 50 000 members (including 18 000 student members) in 130 countries; it provides internationally recognised qualifications both directly and through a network of over 300 study centres; and it has 52 branches, regions and interest groups across the world. Through its contact centre, it engages with 110 000 individuals and has a popular and thriving online presence. Of course, this is not simply a testament to the Institute's efficiency and the popularity of its offer; it is a sign of the enduring significance and power of marketing.

How this book is organised

In developing *The Marketing Century*, the Institute has worked with some of the world's finest and most experienced marketing executives and academics. Each chapter provides a guide to a significant area of marketing, including:

- Strategic marketing
- Segmentation
- Innovation
- Digital marketing
- Sales and business development
- Customer relationship management (CRM)
- Branding
- Advertising
- Public relations
- Internal marketing
- Sustainability
- Social marketing

The development of each subject (for example public relations) is explored, with the first part of each chapter briefly outlining how the subject has developed since its inception and highlighting some of the key milestones. The second part of each chapter is the core. This considers the present situation and explains what is currently 'best practice', what are the cardinal rules, who are the best organisations in this area and what they are doing to ensure success. Crucially, it also indicates how the topic relates to other marketing issues. The benefits of this approach are that it provides a clear, in-depth focus on each aspect of marketing. The final part of each chapter considers the future, exploring the influences that are shaping each aspect of marketing and the trends.

Key themes and developments in marketing

While each chapter examines the past, present and future of marketing, there are several consistent and unifying themes that cut across all of the topics that are part of *The Marketing Century*. In the last 100 years these themes have shaped marketing and, more generally, business life as a whole. They feature in virtually every chapter, albeit in different guises and in different ways. These key themes include the following:

- The inexorable rise of *technology* and its impact both on what customers want and what marketing can achieve. Interestingly, the history of marketing suggests that the impact of technology is often over-estimated in the short term and under-estimated in the long term.
- Related to the rise of technology is the need for *invention and innovation*, a theme that has often been present and is one of the main forces driving competitiveness.
- The spread of *globalisation* and greater global prosperity in the twentieth century, and the value of being both global and local in the twenty-first century.
- Closely linked to globalisation is the need to appreciate difference and the implications of *diversity*, an issue long recognised by marketers and reflected in the concept of *segmentation*.
- Another constant theme is the desire among customers, employees, shareholders and whole societies for an *ethical approach to business*, with greater social awareness and responsibility. Crucially, the need for an ethical approach resembles the need for a clear customer focus: it has to be genuine and felt throughout the organisation.

> The simple truth is that by encouraging a focus on customers, marketing is providing an essential rallying point for everyone in the business.

It cannot simply be 'grafted' on but has to be an integral part of the way things are done.

- The understanding of *behaviour, people and relationships* is now an established mainstay of modern marketing and is an area that has grown rapidly in credibility. Throughout *The Marketing Century* you will see how the issues of trust, engagement, loyalty and connection have become increasingly relevant. Our understanding and experience in this area continue to develop.

- *Managing for the long term* as well as the short term is another recurring theme. Issues of long-term success have been championed by several sources, notably customers, marketers and shareholders. Clearly, the case for developing long-term relationships with customers and providing greater shareholder value through the development of intangible assets (such as brands) is nothing new, but it has been gaining in relevance during the last 100 years – especially during the last 10. This issue also highlights how marketing intersects with a range of issues; so, for example, managing for the long term is facilitated by technology, driven by the need for ethical selling and enhanced by the ability to build relationships.

- The impact of marketing on business *strategy and leadership*. Clearly this is a mutually reinforcing relationship, but marketing has a major effect on issues as wide ranging as innovation, team working, employee engagement, financial management, operational efficiency and many more. One reason for this is that the marketing century has witnessed an increasing understanding of customers and the importance of *customer service and focus*. The simple truth is that by encouraging a focus on customers, marketing is providing an essential rallying point for everyone in the business.

About each chapter

The Marketing Century opens with a clear statement from Don Peppers and Martha Rogers: it is vital that organisations put customers at the heart of what they do, both in the long term and the short term. To create value, firms must lift their sights from the typical focus on current profits and instead start seeing customers as the company's long-term resource – looking at each customer in terms of the long-term return they generate. A long-term strategy for marketing – one that focuses on customer equity and not solely on current profits – can provide marketing with the context and objectives needed to maximise the overall value created by each customer. This is the essence of their chapter, which focuses on *strategic marketing*.

One of marketing's defining concepts, *segmentation*, is explored in Malcolm McDonald's chapter. He explains that all organisations need a better understanding of all their customers and the complexity of the market, and this is where market segmentation is crucial. There is a general lack of understanding about market segmentation and especially the real needs of customers in mature markets. This leads organisations to trade on price and, therefore, makes them behave as if they were in a commodity market. This is the whole point of market segmentation: competing only on price assumes that price is the main requirement of customers, whereas this is rarely the case.

One of the over-arching themes of the last 100 years has been the growing recognition that customers lie at the heart of the organisation's activities and this is reflected in the next chapter about *innovation*, written by John Saunders and Veronica Wong. They explain how innovative companies succeed: what they do to ensure success, the pitfalls they avoid and the lessons that others can learn from them. The challenges of commercialisation and taking new products to market are also described. With the twin forces of globalisation and technology giving rise to some of the most significant, memorable and valuable business developments, innovation is an essential aspect of marketing. It has come to be viewed as equivalent to new product development, but any new activity that improves the organisation by adding value for customers is important.

Technology and advertising feature strongly in the chapter on *digital marketing* by Philip Sheldrake. This was almost too long to write, such is the burgeoning volume of technological opportunities, influences and challenges that are shaping the next marketing century. It is essential because technology is enabling so much modern communication, leading to greater knowledge and understanding. Computers power the internet and modern telecommunications, providing an infrastructure that delivers consumer content, conversations, applications and services. This, in turn, has attracted mass involvement and participation, which has led us to digital marketing and its language of persuasion. Digital marketing encompasses a wide range of platforms, media, channels, tools, services and applications. This chapter provides an expert guide to the past, present and future, highlighting some of the most significant, interesting or impactful developments.

In the chapter on *sales and business development*, Beth Rogers eloquently addresses the fact that selling has often not received the recognition or respect it deserves during the last 100 years. The point is one of extremes: when selling is bad it is ghastly, and when it succeeds and is at its best it is a triumph. However, between these two extremes it is still never less than essential. This chapter provides a fascinating guide to the development of sales, what makes a great sale and salesperson, as well as the changing character of selling. This echoes points made in other chapters and different contexts: selling, like so much in modern marketing, relies on a trusted, ethical approach, innovation and the capacity to build profitable long-term relationships based on a clear understanding of the customer. It is also where 'the rubber hits the road' and connects a wide range of activities in the organisation. For that reason it is both strategic and tactical: an issue that is recognised as being important by everyone from the chief executive to the most junior new recruit.

Merlin Stone's chapter on *customer relationship management* (CRM) takes up the point that customer insights and relationships are a vital, influential component of business success. He explains that the value of CRM lies in its ability to help businesses improve their understanding of their customers. Organisations that do this effectively are more competitive and profitable because they are better able to segment and appeal to different customers, develop and maintain profitable customer relationships, decide how to handle unprofitable customers and customise their offer and promotional efforts. Achieving success often requires sophisticated technology and analytical skills, but by enabling organisations to focus on how they interact with customers, CRM enhances the customer experience and builds long-term customer value.

The concepts of dialogue, understanding and trust form an important element of the next chapter on *branding*. Here, Graham Hales defines a brand as a living asset that is brought to life across all touchpoints, which, if properly managed, creates identification, differentiation and value. Brands matter for many reasons: they raise awareness of a product or service; they show what is distinctive about the product or business; and they convey emotional relevance, making the case for a purchase against other alternatives. The fact that they can influence choices can result in price premiums, loyalty and advocacy that will create revenue and profit for the owner, building brand equity and shareholder value. The evolution of branding is interesting and even today it is a keenly debated subject, perhaps because a brand often conveys what it is that a society values at a given moment in time.

Closely linked with the development of branding is *advertising*, which is explored in the next chapter. Here, Jonathan Gabay makes the point that during the marketing century advertising has changed dramatically: not just in style but in its approach, meaning and substance. What started as a tool controlled by the few to reach the many has undergone a transformation – one that is still happening – with technology enabling consumers to choose the advertising campaigns and brands they allow into their lives. This changing relationship and shift in power require an increasingly sophisticated, subtle approach, one that draws on technology and a clear understanding of people and behaviour. From its earliest days advertising was closely connected with psychology, focusing on influence, persuasion and the benefits of understanding human behaviour.

The forces of technology and globalisation combine with the need for an ethical approach in both life and work in the next chapter, on *public relations*, by Paul Mylrea. Clearly, much has been achieved and gained in 100 years of marketing, but accusations of propaganda and 'spin' have often been in the background of PR, even as its popularity and value have grown. Good public relations remain critical and this insight-

> Just as an individual might engage in a conversation or dialogue to express a view, persuade, influence, enquire, challenge, manage expectations or understand, all the while staying true to their own values, so it is with PR at an organisational level.

ful, intelligent chapter explains that PR is an essential aspect of organisational life because it is about creating dialogue and generating understanding between an organisation and its publics. It facilitates a relationship and enables people to participate in a genuine conversation, with all that implies.

It is the discipline that looks after reputation. Just as an individual might engage in a conversation or dialogue to express a view, persuade, influence, enquire, challenge, manage expectations or understand, all the while staying true to their own values, so it is with PR at an organisational level.

Keith Glanfield's chapter focuses on *internal marketing*. A subject that at one time would have easily been misunderstood is increasingly recognised as being an essential, indispensable way of achieving short-term profits and long-term growth, as well as greater efficiency, brand equity and shareholder value. Marketing can be seen as a single thread that runs throughout the organisation, connecting everything that happens internally with customers and others outside the business. This marketing thread needs to be consistent, it needs to inform and set standards, it needs to be real and present. Above all, it shapes the culture – the way things are done – and this affects key messages, branding, positioning and the way the business appears. Issues of trust, loyalty, customer relationships, perceptions and appeal all benefit from greater internal dialogue, understanding and marketing.

An issue that has always been present but has come to greater prominence relatively recently is *sustainability*. In his chapter, John Grant makes the point that while brand marketing and sustainability are often thought of as opposites (the former urges people to consume more, the latter to consume less), it is far from a simple case of two entirely separate and contradictory domains. Like many cultural opposites, brands and sustainability are intertwined.

In recent years it has become clear that achieving an ethical, sustainable approach to business is one of the most significant challenges ever faced by commercial enterprises, yet potentially one of the most rewarding. Many customers and stakeholders value both a sustainable approach to business and one that is commercially successful. Those forward-thinking organisations that are able to achieve both are finding that the rewards are well worth the effort.

The next chapter, on *social marketing*, explains how marketers tackle some of society's most challenging problems by using commercial marketing practices together with other techniques to change the behaviour and attitudes of individuals – no small task. Veronica Sharp recognises the impact of marketing and the difference it can make: in particular, the fact that it adds genuine value and is increasingly used to improve the quality of people's decisions and lives. For example, to tackle the problems that face society (such as global warming), governmental organisations need marketing campaigns that are capable of achieving real change in people's behaviour.

The concept succeeds by recognising that people do not operate in isolation. Social marketers have to overcome significant barriers to change and deeply ingrained attitudes, often among the most disadvantaged in society. To achieve this, they merge marketing with insights from social science to devise new types of marketing campaign that influence people's behaviour and decisions. To build long-term relationships with customers, organisations need

> Social marketing has much to offer the commercial world, where behavioural change is the gold standard for marketers seeking to develop strong customer relationships.

to gain a full understanding of their customers at a psychological and behavioural level and then know how to make best use of this information. This means offering the products and services that people want and developing messages that will resonate with customers. Far from being contrived or exploitative, social marketing is about understanding people and giving them what they want, or persuading them that what you are asking them to do is in their own interests.

Fittingly, social marketing leaves us with several lessons that can, perhaps, be applied to every aspect of marketing. It is developing fast, often out of all recognition; it can be misunderstood and needs to be managed carefully and in a way that emphasises continuous learning; it is made easier, cheaper and more effective by technology; it helps to build dialogue and trust; it relies on an ethical approach, closely reflect-

> In the marketing century, the need to *learn* about key developments and best practices in marketing, *develop* your thinking, skills and organisation, and *belong* to a network and community of shared interests has never been greater.

ing the times in which we live. And it is essential.

Key questions for the future of marketing

In the future, marketers will need to address fundamental and significant questions in order to realise the full potential for their organisations:

- With the amount of information available to organisations rapidly expanding, how do you ensure that you are using the right information in the right way to gain the best results?
- How is the development of technology changing the way that marketers work in your organisation? Is it simply 'old rules, new tools'? How can technology be used to best effect?
- With the practice of marketing becoming increasingly subtle and complex, how can marketers ensure that they are managing their stakeholders' interests?
- Behavioural change and professional development are vital for marketers in order to develop their skills and expertise; are you doing enough to develop your skills and approach and those of your colleagues?
- Marketing can be viewed as a system of resources interacting and supporting each other – for example reputation, data, marketing capabilities, brand, distribution channels and other elements – and all combining to form a marketing system. How robust is your marketing system? What are the strengths, weaknesses and areas for improvement?

One of the most significant and interesting lessons of the last 100 years is the fact that the future has always been complex, competitive and different. The discipline of marketing has developed and continues to evolve at a fast pace, just as markets, technology and business itself progress. This pace of change and level of complexity are set to increase in the twenty-first century, driven still further by the development of international markets, globalisation and technological change. In these circumstances, the need to *learn* about key developments and best practices in marketing, *develop* your thinking, skills and organisation, and *belong* to a network and community of shared interests has never been greater.

The contributors to this book address the critical questions that are being demanded of our profession. Their expertise is highly valued, appreciated and insightful, and we hope that you continue to enjoy *The Marketing Century*.

Further information

The Institute provides a wide range of resources for marketing professionals at all stages of their careers and is a leading source of market intelligence.

Marketers and members of the Institute can access a wide variety of cutting-edge research papers, market reports and case studies. These include:

- *Original research* – including the latest thinking on marketing topics in the Institute's agenda papers as well as the findings of industry-leading Marketing Trends Surveys.
- *Marketing intelligence library and modelling tools* – these help individuals and businesses to build, refresh and test their marketing approach.
- *Fact files* – these are easy-to-read, downloadable documents providing marketers with the full facts on everything from brand management to marketing law.

Other benefits of membership include an extensive range of full-text journals, dedicated researchers to assist with desk research and a weekly marketing news bulletin.

For further information, please visit www.CIM.co.uk.

Chapter 1

STRATEGIC MARKETING

Don Peppers and Martha Rogers PhD
Founders, Peppers & Rogers Group

Don Peppers and **Martha Rogers** are founding partners of Peppers & Rogers Group, a worldwide management consulting and media firm dedicated to helping clients improve the customer-facing sides of their businesses.

Peppers and Rogers have co-authored many best-selling books that offer new insights on customer strategy and building the value of the customer. They have devised an entirely new way of measuring the value that businesses create. Their latest book *Rules to Break & Laws to Follow: How Your Business Can Beat the Crisis of Short-Termism* shows how to maximise long-term profit by revealing what empowered customers, networked employees, innovation and trust can achieve for businesses.

Marketing's development over the past 100 years has been dynamic, delivering to enterprises genuine value from a wide range of benefits, including branding, customer relationships, innovation, and digital and social marketing. This dynamism has also produced significant challenges in promoting, selling and distributing products and services, challenges that stem from long-standing, but flawed, assumptions about how enterprises create real shareholder value. A long-term strategy for marketing – one that focuses on customer equity and not solely on current profits – can provide marketing with the context and objectives needed to maximise the overall value created by each customer. This is strategic marketing.

The past is … past

Marketing strategy has too often been shaped by the need to imitate what worked in the past, what has been perceived to be successful for other companies or what is currently generating revenue for the company. Decision makers within enterprises review case studies and pursue best-practice guidance centred on the historical success of other companies, and while these behaviours can be reasonable adaptive approaches to the delivery of success, they function as default mechanisms. This behavioural mimicry is hard to overcome. However, our research and experience suggest that mimicking what worked for immediate profits in the past now leads businesses to settle for less and to make irrational decisions that overlook chances for real growth.

The unrelenting pressure to make concrete numbers right now submerges the instinct to do what is 'right for the company' and stalls forward-thinking business intelligence, eroding the long-term value of customer-first marketing strategies. We call this management development the crisis of short-termism.

Strategic marketing is future-oriented, requiring energy and the ability to balance hard, rational analysis with soft skills such as creativity. It also requires flexibility and the capacity to learn and change. Our suggestion to twenty-first-century business executives who seek to avoid the crisis of short-termism is to consider making a change in their mental model of success, for both quarterly numbers and long-term financial results. Whether you are running a complicated business, developing the marketing strategy for that business, or conducting a marketing campaign, two straightforward principles for the model are that a) customer trust is an indisputable element for future business success; and b) employees' trust in the company is fundamental to their commitment to earning your customers' trust.

The fallacy of short-term thinking

The fundamental task for marketing in the twenty-first century is to help businesses triumph over the fallacy of short-term thinking that seems to erode corporate performance at all levels. We identify some of these flawed assumptions about marketing as rules to break. Some of the truths we've learnt about long-term business thinking we call laws to follow, which we expand on later in this chapter. Most important for now, more than any other issue, is that these rules to break and laws to follow all point to the crisis of short-termism and how to make sure your company is not part of it.

It is tempting to believe that the best measures, or rules, for business success are a company's current sales and profits; that the right sales and marketing efforts will always get a company more customers; and that company value is created by offering differentiated products and services. These are assumptions about how a business thrives that are tied to the past, and they simply don't work any more. The speed and scope of technological innovation in the past two decades, particularly in the areas of analytics, interactivity and mass customisation, have made formerly accurate, useful and reasonable marketing assumptions obsolete. Adhering to these false assumptions leads to short-termism, a way of thinking that, rather than creating more value, ensnares companies in a cycle of value destruction. Businesses become obsessively focused on short-term shareholder value, revenue and profit at the expense of longer-term returns and the overall future value of the company.

Short-termism and the Return on Customer metric

Business history is full of examples of once-great companies that managed for the short term and as a result no longer exist (or are certainly no longer as great as they once were). Sometimes short-termism results from simple complacency: a belief that the firm is 'too large to fail', or that it is so venerated that the future will simply look after itself. At other times, short-termism is bred by outright fraud and corruption, as happened in the cases of Enron and Ameriquest.

Strategic marketing plays an essential role in capturing the greatest benefits for an organisation by developing a corporate culture and focus that look at each customer not only in terms of immediate profit to be generated, but also in terms of long-term value to be created.

Companies are tempted to – and frequently do – concentrate on short-term profit, because poor earnings numbers have serious repercussions for an enterprise's share price and the ability to raise investment, calling the business's future into question. The problem is that the narrow focus of short-termism does not maximise profits by thoroughly tapping customer loyalty and satisfaction opportunities, but instead leads to customer churn, which destroys loyalty and strengthens competitors while raising customer acquisition and maintenance costs and lowering profitability. Strategic marketing is based on accurate, relevant measurements that better reveal where a company's true value lies and it therefore mandates a balance of short-term success and long-term value building. It is essential to assess the return from each customer – what we call Return on Customer (ROC).

The ROC metric is a vital part of valuing a company's financial potential and determining strategic marketing priorities to realise that potential. ROC measures the value that a business creates or destroys with its actions, and ROC-efficient companies take action to build and maintain their Customer Equity (CE).

The ROC equation

The long-term value of customers is often both poorly understood and improperly quantified. The best businesses operate as though customers are scarce and markets are

> The Return on Customer metric is a vital part of valuing a company's financial potential and determining strategic marketing priorities to realise that potential. ROC measures the value that a business creates or destroys with its actions.

competitive. To obtain maximum lifetime value from each customer, enterprises need to adopt an approach to marketing strategy that incorporates all areas of a business, but the most important territory to manage is how companies win and lose the trust of customers. ROC equals a firm's current-period cash flow from its customers plus any changes in the underlying Customer Equity (CE), divided by the total CE at the beginning of the period.

The Return on Customer equation

Return on Customer can be calculated as follows:

$$ROC = \frac{\Pi_i + \Delta CE_i}{CE_{i-1}}$$

Where Π_i = Cash flow from customers during period i

ΔCE_i = change in customer equity during period *i*

CE_{i-1} = customer equity at the beginning of period *i*

This calculation requires us to define what we mean by CE, which, unlike the tangible business asset of capital, is seen as an intangible business asset. A company's value, aside from its capital assets, relies on the sum total of its customers' combined lifetime value (LTV), a fact that by itself can help to determine how CE is used, consumed, altered and replenished in the course of business. It is necessary to keep in mind that there exists no fixed set of customers for enterprises to depend on, no guaranteed patronage pattern; customers can change their minds at any time about what to consume and how much of their money they spend doing so. It is companies' own actions that influence the future behaviour of their existing and prospective customers, and CE depends on every customer interaction being viewed as an opportunity to increase the customer's lifetime value.

Customer equity can be estimated by adding the future revenue stream received from each customer (a customer's lifetime value, or LTV) and adding to it all the lifetime values of current and future customers. By calculating the ROC, businesses will better know where they need to concentrate their resources and where they need to improve. Also, by knowing the potential future cash flows a customer is likely to generate over time, companies will know if the level of investment involved in acquiring that customer is justified.

The link between shareholder return and ROC is impossible to avoid: ROC measures the value that a business creates or destroys with its actions, and ROC-efficient companies build and maintain their CE. Essentially, they are two ways of looking at the same thing: how to maximise potential profit.

Key questions about strategic marketing

- How does your company create value? How do your competitors?
- How could you deliver even greater value for your customers?
- How well do you and your colleagues know your customers? How strong are your customer relationships?
- Do you measure the Return on Customer? Do you see the value of a customer beyond the current purchase they have made? What do you do to get the customer to buy from you in the future?
- Does your business have the right balance between achieving short-term results and planning for the long term? How could this improve?

Chapter 2

MARKET SEGMENTATION

Malcolm McDonald

Emeritus Professor at Cranfield University School of Management and Honorary Professor at Warwick Business School

Professor **Malcolm McDonald** is Emeritus Professor at Cranfield University School of Management and Honorary Professor at Warwick Business School. He has written over 40 books, including the best seller *Marketing Plans: How to Prepare Them, How to Use Them*, and he has authored over one hundred articles and papers. He is one of the world's leading marketing experts, combining academic rigour and commercial application to provide organisations with solutions for strategic marketing and marketing planning, market segmentation, key account management, international marketing and marketing accountability. He is currently chairman of six companies and works with the operating boards of a number of the world's leading multi-nationals on all continents.

After 50 years, market segmentation is still at the heart of successful marketing. This chapter is in three parts. The first part summarises research into market segmentation and its development. The second part is a practitioner-oriented view of how segmentation can be used to ensure success. The third part briefly discusses the future of market segmentation.

The development of market segmentation

The father of market segmentation is widely considered to be Wendell Smith, who proposed market segmentation as an alternative to product differentiation. Yet it wasn't until Yoram Wind's (1978) review of the state of market segmentation that the topic went to the top of the agenda of researchers and practitioners. His plea was for new segmentation bases, for data-analysis techniques and generally for putting market segmentation at the heart of strategic decision making.

In 2009, a whole issue of the *Journal of Marketing Management* was devoted to market segmentation. The articles confirm that most of the work over the intervening years has been primarily around what segmentation bases to use, such as size of purchase, customer characteristics, product attributes, benefits sought, service quality, buying behaviour and, more recently, propensity to switch suppliers, with much of this work being biased towards fast-moving consumer goods, rather than to business-to-business and services.

Unfortunately, much of the academic debate about market segmentation can be seen as somewhat arrogant and inward looking. The justification for saying this is that anyone who says 'we segment markets by ...' is totally missing the point. Any market, once correctly defined in terms of needs rather than products, consists entirely of what is bought, how it is used and why it is bought

Any market, once defined in terms of needs rather than products, consists entirely of what is bought, how it is used and why it is bought and used in these ways. The role of any supplier is to understand these behavioural patterns and to discover their rationale.

Table 2.1 Characteristics of excellent and weak marketing strategies

Excellent Strategies	Weak Strategies
Target needs-based segments	Target product categories
Make a specific offer to each segment	Make similar offers to all segments
Leverage their strengths and minimise their weaknesses	Have little understanding of their strengths and weaknesses
Anticipate the future	Plan using historical data

and used in these ways. The role of any supplier is to understand these behavioural patterns and to discover their rationale, rather than trying to impose some predetermined segmentation methodology onto the market.

This chapter briefly explains what is wrong with existing methodologies for segmentation and then outlines a successful, proven, market-based approach. This approach has worked successfully in every sector in which it has been applied during the past 25 years. Research during this period established a vital link between creating shareholder value and achieving excellence in marketing – and this link is shown in the left-hand column of Table 2.1.

Defining the market

It has become clear after at least 70 years of formalised marketing that market definition and segmentation are the very core of the discipline. For example, correct market definition is crucial for:

- Measuring market share
- Measuring growth
- Specifying target customers
- Recognising relevant competitors
- Formulating market strategy.

How to measure market share has always been at the centre of controversy in discussions of failure. Defining a market too broadly or too

A market is the aggregation of all products or services that customers regard as being capable of satisfying the same need.

narrowly can both lead to meaningless statistics. There is one definition that is particularly useful: a market is the aggregation of all products or services that customers regard as being capable of satisfying the same need. Companies frequently confuse target markets with products – pensions or mainframe computers, for example. This, coupled with a lack of knowledge about the sources of differential advantage in each segment, signals trouble.

Many companies pride themselves on their market segmentation even though these so-called segments are in fact *sectors*, which is a common misconception. Everyone with a marketing qualification knows that a segment is a group of customers with the same or similar needs and that there are many different purchase combinations within and across sectors.

However, the gravest mistake of all is *a priori* segmentation. Most books incorrectly state that there are several bases for segmentation, such as socio-economics, demographics, geo-demographics and the like, but this misses the point completely. For example, Boy George and the Archbishop of Canterbury are both members of socio-economic group A, but they don't behave the same. Equally, all 18–24-year-old women do not

> Companies frequently confuse target markets with products and lack knowledge about the sources of differential advantage within each segment.

behave the same way, despite being part of the same demographic segment.

In truth, it is the way in which goods and services are made, distributed and used and the resulting purchase combinations that comprise an actual market. So, the task for marketers has been to understand market structure and how a market works, and to identify the different purchase combinations (segments). Approaches such as socio-economics, demographics, geo-demographics and psychographics are clearly extremely useful at a very high level of marketing. For example, young married couples will represent a large group who have a need for furniture, but within this substantial group there will clearly be several different need sets, known as segments.

Why segmentation matters

The importance of market segmentation is highlighted by considering the following situation. When something new is invented, not everyone adopts it at the same time. Many years ago an American researcher, Everett Rogers, studied how new products diffuse across markets over time (Rogers expressed this in his *Diffusion of Innovation* curve; for further information see Rogers, 1995). For example, imagine that television has just been invented. Let us also imagine that there are only 100 households in a country. Assuming that each household will only want one television, the potential market for televisions is therefore 100. However, not everyone will buy a television at the same time. Someone (or some group) has to be the first to adopt new products. Normally, about 2.5 per cent of any population will be the first to adopt new products. These people are known as *Innovators*, and they tend to enjoy being different.

Innovators are followed by another group, known as *Opinion Leaders*. These people tend to be affluent, well-educated, very privileged and independent thinkers. Often, they do not care much what other people think of them. This group is crucial in getting any new product or service adopted. Opinion Leaders are followed by a much larger group known as the *Early Majority*. These people admire the Opinion Leaders and aim to emulate them. When these people start to enter a market, there is a rapid growth in sales.

By now, approximately 50 per cent of all those who could adopt the new product have done so, and it is here that the *Late Majority* begin to enter the market. Generally, these people are less privileged, less affluent and less well educated. At this stage, price often becomes very important. Finally, the remaining 16 per cent of the population adopt the new technology. Everett Rogers refers to these people as *Laggards*. By now, everyone who could have a television has got one. At this stage, companies can be facing a replacement market where growth will be dependent on issues such as population size and demographics. Clearly, in mature markets, achieving growth is much more difficult.

This brief foray into Rogers' diffusion of innovation curve reveals who the Opinion Leaders are in a market. This matters when launching a new product or service, as these people should be targeted first by the sales force and then by other promotional media, as they will be the most likely to

> All organisations need to understand all of their customers and the complexity of the market, and this is where market segmentation is crucial.

respond. For example, certain doctors will be more open-minded about new drugs, whereas other doctors will not risk prescribing a new drug until it has been on the market for a number of years. The diffusion of innovation curve also highlights the product's lifecycle, which enables marketers to know what strategy is best to deploy at each stage of the product's lifecycle.

All organisations need to better understand all of their customers and the complexity of the market, and this is where market segmentation is crucial. As demand grows rapidly with the entry of the Early Majority, it is common for new competitors to offer variations on early models. This gives consumers greater choice. At this stage, markets break into smaller groups. As markets mature, and there is more supply than demand, growth tends to be in the lower-priced end of the market, while the top end of the market tends to be immune. It is usually the middle market that suffers at this stage, with many competitors vying with each other on price.

This is the whole point of market segmentation: competing only on price assumes that price is the main requirement of customers, whereas this is rarely the case. There is a general lack of understanding about market segmentation and especially the real needs of customers in mature markets. This leads organisations to

> Competing only on price assumes that price is the main requirement of customers, whereas this is rarely the case.

trade on price and, therefore, makes them behave as if they were in a commodity market.

How markets segment

Let us examine the factors that cause markets to break into smaller groups. In Western Europe and other advanced economies, most consumers have televisions, washing machines, cars and the like. So, for example, if Ford wants to grow sales of its vehicles, it can no longer rely on the kind of market growth we have all enjoyed since 1945. Today it has to take sales from a competitor, which means that it has to pay very close attention to consumer needs – and this is why market segmentation matters.

Clearly, in the early days, markets will tend to be homogeneous. However, as demand grows rapidly with the entry of the Early Majority, it is common for new entrants to offer variations on the early models and consumers now have a choice. The starting point in market segmentation is correct market definition, which is crucial for measuring market size, growth and share, identifying relevant competitors and formulating strategies to deliver differential advantage. Few companies give sufficient attention to correct market definition and few can draw an accurate market map. As a result, they have little chance of doing anything remotely resembling correct market segmentation at the key influence points or junctions on the map. At each of these junctions, segmentation is not only possible but crucial. (The methodology for market segmentation is explained fully in McDonald & Dunbar, 2007.)

The difference between customers and consumers

As marketing has developed in complexity so, too, has the question of exactly who is a customer. Clearly, resolving this issue is a vital prerequisite for successful segmentation. Let us start with the difference between customers and consumers. The term 'consumer' is interpreted by most people to mean the final consumer, who is not necessarily the customer. Take the example of a mother or father who is buying breakfast cereals. The chances are that they are intermediate customers acting as agents on behalf of the eventual consumers (their family). In order to market cereals effectively, it is clearly necessary to understand what the family wants as well as what the parents want.

The consumer is the final user of the product, who is not necessarily the customer. It is clearly necessary to understand what the end-consumer wants, as well as what the purchaser wants. Also, there can be several intermediary customers before the end-consumer is reached. At each stage of production, the end-user must always be considered and we must be alert to any changes in their consumption patterns. Clearly, we not only need to identify our immediate customers, we need to broaden our view of who our customers are. A common mistake is to focus just on the customers who purchase directly from us.

Recognising your customers

Given the distinction between customers and consumers and the need continually to be alert to any changes in the consumption patterns of the products in the market, the next question to be faced is: Who are our customers?

Direct customers are those people or organisations who buy directly from us. They could, therefore, be distributors, retailers and the like. However, there is a tendency for organisations to confine their interest (and their marketing) only to those who actually place orders. This can be a major mistake, as can be seen from the following case history.

A fertiliser company that had grown and prospered during the 1970s and 1980s because of the superior nature of its products reached its farmer consumers via merchants (wholesalers). However, as other companies copied the technology, the merchants began to stock competitive products and drove prices and margins down. Had the fertiliser company paid more attention to the needs of its different farmer groups and developed products especially for them, based on farmer segmentation, it would have continued to create demand pull through differentiation.

A segmentation study revealed that there were seven distinct types of farmer, each with a different set of needs. For example, there was a segment we called Arthur, who bought on price alone but represented only 10 per cent of the market, not the 100 per cent put about by everyone in the industry, especially the sales force.

Another type of farmer we called Oliver, who would drive around his fields on his tractor with an aerial linked to a satellite and an on-board computer. He did this in order to analyse the soil type and would then mix P, N and K, which are the principal ingredients of fertiliser, solely to get the maximum yield out of his farm. In other words, Oliver was a scientific farmer, but the supply industry believed he was buying on price because he bought his own ingredients as cheaply as possible. He did this, however, only because none of the suppliers bothered to understand his needs.

Another type of farmer we called David, who was a show-off and liked his crops to look nice and healthy. He also liked his cows to have nice, healthy skins. Clearly, if a sales representative had talked in a technical way to David, he would quickly have switched off. Equally, to talk about the appearance of crops and livestock would have turned Oliver off, but this is the whole point. Every single supplier in the industry totally ignored the real needs of these farmers, and the only thing anyone ever talked about was price.

The result was a market driven by price discounts, accompanied by substantial losses to the suppliers. ICI, however, armed with this new-found information, launched new products and new promotional approaches aimed at these different farmer types and achieved immediate results, becoming the most profitable subsidiary of the ICI group and the only profitable fertiliser company in the country.

Understanding market dynamics and market share

Let us now return to market dynamics and what happens to markets at the rapid growth stage. At this point, new competitors enter the market attracted by high sales and high profits. For example, in the early 1970s, one photocopier company had an 80 per cent market share and massive profit margins. When a Japanese newcomer (Canon) entered the market with small photocopiers, the giant ignored it. The Japanese product grew in popularity, forcing the giant to reduce its prices. Within three years, the giant's share was down to 10 per cent and the battle was lost. It had failed to recognise that the market was segmented and tried to compete in all segments with it main product – a common mistake made by market leaders. The point is that companies should not attempt to compete in all segments with the same product, but should recognise that different segments (or groups with different needs) develop as the market grows. Organisations should develop appropriate products and services and then position them accordingly.

There are at least four major changes that occur over a product's lifecycle and these can be seen in Figure 2.1. The far right-hand column shows the 'commodity' stage, where the market has matured for a particular product and profit margins can fall. This, however, is by no means inevitable, and only occurs in markets where organisations do not understand the power of market segmentation. There are other options, of course, including getting out of mature markets or moving the goal posts – approaches successfully applied by such businesses as First Direct, Dell, Direct Line and Amazon.com. However, as markets mature, the strategy that should be considered first is market segmentation.

Key concept

Defining markets in terms of customer needs

Correct market definition is crucial for several reasons: measuring market share and market growth; the specification of target customers; recognition of relevant competitors; and, most important of all, the formulation of marketing strategy. It is this, above all else, that delivers differential advantage.

The general rule for 'market' definition is that it should be described in terms of a customer need in a way that covers the aggregation of all the products or services that customers regard as being capable of satisfying the same need. For example, we would regard the in-company caterer as only one option when it came to satisfying lunchtime hunger. This particular need could also be satisfied at external restaurants, public houses, fast food specialists and sandwich bars. The emphasis in the definition, therefore, is clearly on the word 'need'.

The product / market life cycle and market characteristics

Key Characteristics	Unique	Product Differentiation	Service Differentiation	'Commodity'
Marketing Message	Explain	Competitive	Brand Values	Corporate
Sales	Pioneering	Relative Benefits Distribution Support	Relationship Based	Availability Based
Distribution	Direct Selling	Exclusive Distribution	Mass Distribution	80 : 20
Price	Very High	High	Medium	Low (Consumer Controlled)
Competitive Intensity	None	Few	Many	Fewer, bigger International
Costs	Very High	Medium	Medium/Low	Very low
Profit	Medium/High	High	Medium/High	Medium/low
Management Style	Visionary	Strategic	Operational	Cost Management

Figure 2.1 The product/market lifecycle and market characteristics

An excellent example is provided by Procter & Gamble in the USA supplying Wal-Mart, the giant food retailer. P&G creates demand pull (with high turnover and high margins) by paying detailed attention to both the needs of end-consumers and the needs of its direct customer (Wal-Mart). Wal-Mart is able to operate on very low margins because it is only when the barcode of a product is scanned at the till that P&G invoices for it, produces another product and activates the distribution chain. This is done through an integrated IT process. This has reduced Wal-Mart's costs by hundreds of millions of dollars.

The state of the art: Making market segmentation work

We can now begin to concentrate on a methodology for making market segmentation a reality, market segmentation being the means by which any company seeks to gain a differential advantage over its competitors.

Markets usually fall into natural groups, or segments, which contain customers who exhibit a similar level of interest in the same broad requirements. These segments form separate markets in themselves and can often be of considerable size. Taken to its extreme, each individual consumer is a unique market segment, because all people are different in their requirements. While CRM systems have made it possible to engage in one-to-one communications, this in not viable in most organisations unless economies of scale have been obtained at a higher level of aggregation, such as at segment level. Consequently, products are made to appeal to groups of customers who share approximately the same needs.

It is not surprising, then, to hear that there are certain universally accepted criteria concerning what constitutes a viable market segment:

- Segments should be of an adequate size to provide the company with the desired return for its effort
- Members of each segment should have a high degree of similarity in their requirements, yet be distinct from the rest of the market
- Criteria for describing segments must enable the company to communicate effectively with them

While many of these criteria may appear obvious, in practice market segmentation is one of the most difficult marketing concepts to turn into a reality. Yet we must succeed, otherwise we become just another company selling 'me too' products. In other words, what we offer the potential customer is very much the same as what any other company offers and, in such circumstances, it is likely to be the lowest priced article that is bought. This can be ruinous to our profits, unless we happen to have lower costs, hence higher margins, than our competitors.

The three stages of market segmentation

There are three essential stages to market segmentation, all of which have to be completed.

1 The first stage establishes the scope of the project and defines the market. This stage also looks at the way the market operates and identifies where purchasing decisions are made. Successful segmentation is based on a detailed understanding of these decision makers (customers and end-users) and their requirements.
2 The second stage assesses the way customers actually behave in the marketplace. It answers the question 'Who is specifying what?'.
3 The third stage looks at the reasons behind the behaviour of customers in the marketplace, addressing the question 'Why?' before searching for market segments based on this analysis of needs.

Stage 1: Defining the market

The first step in market segmentation establishes the scope of the segmentation by specifying the relevant geographical area and by clearly understanding, from a customer's perspective, the 'market' in which your products or services are competing with those of your competitors. Where necessary, the scope is modified to take into account the realistic capabilities of your organisation.

A clear geographical boundary enables you to establish the size of the market, to identify the localities in which the dynamics of the market have to be understood and, once the segments have been identified, to develop the appropriate marketing objectives and strategies for those localities.

Keeping the project within the borders of a single country is a manageable starting point, because the stage of market development, the available routes to market and the pattern of marketing activity will probably be the same throughout the country. Even this, however, may be too broad for some companies, simply because their geographical reach is limited by physical or economic considerations, or even because their appeal has a strong local sentiment attached to it.

For companies trading in numerous countries around the world, there is clearly an enormous attraction in finding a single global segmentation

> Successful segmentation is based on a detailed understanding of decision makers (customers and end-users) and their requirements.

model that can be applied to every country. However, the experience of 'globalisation' has highlighted for many of these companies that they have to 'act local' in order to succeed in their market. This doesn't mean that every country is unique in respect of the segments found within it. For an international company, a useful guide to predetermining which countries can be included in a single segmentation project is to ensure that in each of these countries the stage of market development, the available routes to market and the pattern of marketing activity are the same, or at least very similar.

As a reminder, the general rule for 'market' definition is that it should be described in a way that covers the aggregation of all the alternative products or services that customers regard as being capable of satisfying that same need. An example is given in Table 2.2.

Market mapping

A useful way of identifying where decisions are made about competing products and services, and, therefore, those who then proceed to the next stages of segmentation, is to start by drawing a 'market map'.

A market map (Figure 2.2) defines the distribution and value-added chain between final users and suppliers of the products or services included within the scope of your segmentation project. This should take into account the various buying mechanisms found in your market, including the part played by 'influencers'.

Table 2.2 An example of markets and needs from financial services

Market	Need
Emergency cash ('rainy day')	Cash to cover an undesired and unexpected event, often the loss of/damage to property
Future event planning	Schemes to protect and grow money that are for anticipated and unanticipated events (e.g. car replacement/repairs, education, weddings, funerals, health care)
Asset purchase	Cash to buy required assets (e.g. car purchase, house purchase, once-in-a-lifetime holiday)
Welfare contingency	The ability to maintain a desired standard of living for oneself and/or dependants in times of unplanned cessation of salary
Retirement income	The ability to maintain a desired standard of living for oneself and/or dependants once the salary has ceased
Wealth care and building	The care and growth of assets (with various risk and liquidity levels)
Day-to-day money management	The ability to store and readily access cash for day-to-day requirements
Personal financial protection and security from motor vehicle incidents	Car insurance

It is useful to start your market map by plotting the various stages that occur along the distribution and value-added chain, between the final users and all the suppliers of products or services competing with one another in the defined market. At the same time, indicate the particular routes to market the products are sourced through, as not all of them will necessarily involve all of these stages.

The easiest junction at which to start this page of market mapping is at the final users' junction, noting at each junction with leverage the volume/ value (or percentage of the total market) that is decided there. Guesstimate these figures if they are not known and note this as a requirement for any follow-up work.

Market mapping

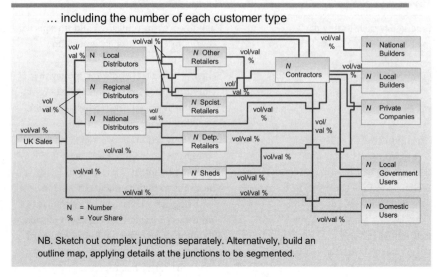

Figure 2.2 A generic market map

Stage 2: Understanding who specifies what, where, when and how

The second stage of market segmentation is to do the following:

- Develop a representative sample of different decision makers
- Identify the characteristics and properties of a purchase on which decisions are made
- Highlight the customer attributes that will be used to describe the decision makers.

Each constituent of this sample is called a 'micro-segment'. The uniqueness of a micro-segment is that when determining which of the alternative offers is to be bought, the decision makers it represents demonstrate a similar level of interest in a specific set of features, with the features being the characteristics and properties of 'what' is bought, 'where' it is bought, 'when' it is bought and 'how' it is bought as appropriate to the micro-segment. To this are added the descriptors, which describe who the micro-segment represents

The market segmentation process

Figure 2.3 The main steps in the market segmentation process

along with an estimate of the volume or value for which they account in the defined market.

The principle behind this step is that by observing the purchase behaviour of decision makers and by understanding the key constituents of this behaviour, we have a platform for developing a detailed understanding of their motivations. It is, therefore, a critical link with the next step of the segmentation process, which looks at why decision makers select the particular products and services they specify. This, in turn, becomes the basis on which the segments are formed.

The process chart in Figure 2.3 describes the main steps in the market segmentation process.

We can now turn to the process again, and move to steps 2, 3, 4 and 5. Essentially, these time-consuming steps involve listing all purchase combinations that take place in the market, including:

- Different applications for the product or service
- Principal forms such as size, colour, branded, unbranded etc.

- Principal channels used, when (e.g. yearly, weekly) and how (e.g. cash or credit).

Next, it is important to describe who behaves in each particular way, using relevant descriptors such as demographics. For industrial purchases this might be standard industrial classifications or size of firm, whereas for consumer purchases this might be socio-economic groups such as A, B, C1, C2, D and E, or the stage reached in the lifecycle, or age, sex, geography, lifestyles or psychographic profiles.

Finally, and most difficult of all, each purchase combination has to have a brief explanation of the reason for this particular type of behaviour. In other words, we need to list the benefits that are sought. It is often at this stage that an organisation needs to pause and either commission market research or refer to its extant database of previous market research studies. Figure 2.4 shows the key components of a micro-segment and, although only ten micro-

Cranfield UNIVERSITY
School of Management

Micro-segments

Micro-segment	1	2	3	4	5	6	7	8	9	10
What is bought										
Where										
When										
And How										
Who										
Why (benefits sought)										

Figure 2.4 Developing micro-segments

segments are shown, it is normal in most markets for companies to identify as many as 30 different micro-segments. Remember, these micro-segments are actual purchase combinations that take place in a market.

Once the work has been done to describe the micro-segments (steps 2, 3, 4 and 5), any good statistical computer program can complete a cluster analysis to arrive at a smaller number of segments. The final step consists of:

> Market segmentation is fundamental to corporate strategy. It is also clear that, since market segmentation affects every single corporate activity, it should not only be an exercise that takes place within the marketing department, and has to involve other functions. Finally, the most senior levels of management must lead this initiative if their organisation is to be truly driven by market or customer needs.

- Checking whether the resulting segments are big enough to justify separate treatment
- Verifying that the segments are sufficiently different from other segments
- Making sure that the segments have been described sufficiently well to enable customers in each segment to be reached
- Getting ready to make the necessary changes to meet the needs of the identified segments.

Clearly, there will be very few markets in the world where all customers have the same needs. Also, once market segmentation has been carried out, it is relatively easy to position products and services to meet the different needs of various segments. The difficult part is segmenting markets. Also, it is vital to focus on serving the needs of the identified segments, while it is dangerous to straddle different segments with the same offer.

The process of market segmentation itself consists of five steps (see Table 2.3).

Market structure and market segmentation are the heart and soul of marketing. Unless an organisation devotes sufficient time and energy to the challenge, driven from the board downwards, it is virtually impossible for it to be market driven. This matters, because in any organisation that is not market driven, the marketing function will be ineffective or, at best, will spend

Table 2.3 Understanding market segmentation

Not all customers in a broadly defined market have the same needs.

Positioning is easy. Market segmentation is difficult. Positioning problems stem from poor segmentation.

Select a segment and serve it. Do not straddle segments and sit between them.

1 Define the market to be segmented and size it (market scope).
2 Determine how the market works and identify who makes the decisions (market mapping).
3 Develop a representative sample of decision makers based on the differences they see as key (including what, where, when and how), note who they are (demographics) and size them.
4 Understand their real needs = (why they buy, the benefits sought).
5 Search for groups with similar needs.

its time trying to promote and sell products or services that are inappropriate for the market.

To summarise, the objectives of market segmentation are:

- To help determine the direction of marketing through the analysis and understanding of trends and buyer behaviour
- To help determine realistic and obtainable marketing and sales objectives
- To help improve decision making by forcing managers to consider in depth the options ahead.

The future of market segmentation

Many of the initiatives introduced over the past 20 years, such as total quality management, business process reengineering, balanced scorecards and knowledge management, have 'failed' in the sense of not living up to expectations. This failure invariably originates from the inability of organisations adopting these initiatives to understand their markets and, crucially, the needs of customers within segments in these markets. This is a vital precursor to developing offers to meet these needs. Without this foundation, all of these excellent initiatives amount to little more than fads adopted as a kind of cure-

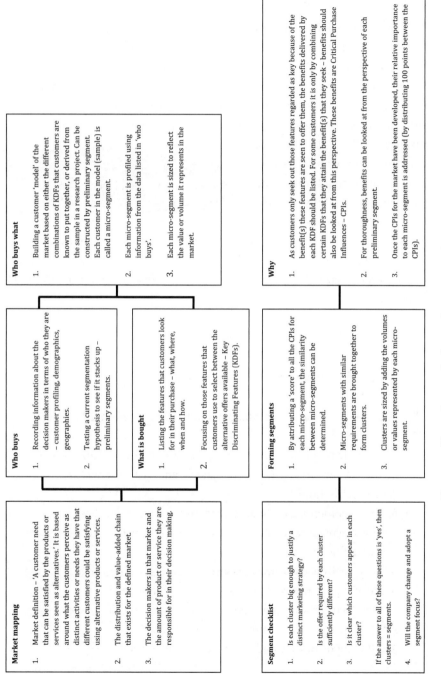

Market mapping

1. Market definition – 'A customer need that can be satisfied by the products or services seen as alternatives.' It is based around what the customers perceive as distinct activities or needs they have that different customers could be satisfying using alternative products or services.

2. The distribution and value-added chain that exists for the defined market.

3. The decision makers in that market and the amount of product or service they are responsible for in their decision making.

Who buys

1. Recording information about the decision makers in terms of who they are – customer profiling, demographics, geographies.

2. Testing a current segmentation hypothesis to see if it stacks up – preliminary segments.

What is bought

1. Listing the features that customers look for in their purchase – what, where, when and how.

2. Focusing on those features that customers use to select between the alternative offers available – Key Discriminating Features (KDFs).

Who buys what

1. Building a customer 'model' of the market based on either the different combinations of KDFs that customers are known to put together, or derived from the sample in a research project. Can be constructed by preliminary segment. Each customer in the model (sample) is called a micro-segment.

2. Each micro-segment is profiled using information from the data listed in 'who buys'.

3. Each micro-segment is sized to reflect the value or volume it represents in the market.

Forming segments

1. By attributing a 'score' to all the CPIs for each micro-segment, the similarity between micro-segments can be determined.

2. Micro-segments with similar requirements are brought together to form clusters.

3. Clusters are sized by adding the volumes or values represented by each micro-segment.

Segment checklist

1. Is each cluster big enough to justify a distinct marketing strategy?

2. Is the offer required by each cluster sufficiently different?

3. Is it clear which customers appear in each cluster?

If the answer to all of these questions is 'yes', then clusters = segments.

4. Will the company change and adopt a segment focus?

Why

1. As customers only seek out those features regarded as key because of the benefit(s) these features are seen to offer them, the benefits delivered by each KDF should be listed. For some customers it is only by combining certain KDFs that they attain the benefit(s) that they seek – benefits should also be looked at from this perspective. These benefits are Critical Purchase Influences – CPIs.

2. For thoroughness, benefits can be looked at from the perspective of each preliminary segment.

3. Once the CPIs for the market have been developed, their relative importance to each micro-segment is addressed (by distributing 100 points between the CPIs).

Figure 2.5 The main steps in the market segmentation process

all for commercial ills and it is not surprising that in such circumstances they often disappoint. Proving this point is the fact that all of these initiatives have worked extremely well in those companies that have been truly market driven.

We are now at a crucial crossroads for the future of marketing. In the UK, for example, few practitioners are professionally qualified. The Chartered Institute of Marketing sits at the very epicentre of marketing education, not just in the UK but globally, with 300 study centres in 132 countries. Qualification through the CIM remains the only sensible solution to the malaise that lies

> 'Segment or die' will be the mantra in the second decade of the twenty-first century.

at the centre of the marketing discipline, with fewer than one in twenty practitioners being professionally qualified. Market segmentation lies at the heart of successful marketing practice and is a core discipline within the CIM syllabus.

Key questions about market segmentation

- Is there a clear and unambiguous definition of the market you are serving?
- Is it clearly mapped, showing product/service flows, volumes/values in total, your shares, decision makers and critical conclusions for your organisation?
- Are the segments clearly described and quantified? (These must be groups of customers with the same or similar needs, not sectors or demographic groups.)
- Are the real needs of these segments properly quantified, with the relative importance of these needs clearly identified?
- Is there a clear and quantified analysis of how well your company satisfies these needs compared to competitors?
- Are the opportunities and threats clearly identified by segment?

continued on next page...

- Are all the segments classified according to their relative potential for growth in profits over the next three years and according to your company's relative competitive position in each?
- Are the objectives consistent with their position in the portfolio? (Consider volume, value, market share and profit.)
- Are the strategies (including products, price, place and services) consistent with these objectives?
- Are the key issues for action for all departments clearly spelt out as key issues to be addressed?
- Do the objectives and strategies add up to the profit goals required by your company?
- Does the budget follow on logically from all of the above, or is it merely an add-on?

References and further information

Bailey, C., Baines, P., Wilson, H. & Clark, M. (2009) Segmentation and customer insight in contemporary services marketing practice: Why grouping customers is no longer enough, *Journal of Marketing Management* 25(3–4): 228–51.

Christensen, C., Cook, S. & Hall, T. (2005) Marketing malpractice: The cause and the cure, *Harvard Business Review* 83(12, December): 74–83.

Coviello, N., Brodie, R., Danacher, P. & Johnston, W. (2002) How firms relate to their markets: An empirical examination of contemporary marketing practice, *Journal of Marketing* 66(3): 33–46.

Jenkins, M. & McDonald, M. (1997) Market segmentation: Organisational archetypes and a research agenda, *European Journal of Marketing* 31(1): 17–30.

McDonald, M. (2004) Marketing existential malpractice and an etherised discipline: A soteriological comment, *Journal of Marketing Management* 20(3–4, April): 387–408.

McDonald, M. & Dunbar, I. (2007) *Market Segmentation: How to Do It; How to Profit from It*, 2nd edn, Oxford: Butterworth-Heinemann.

Rigby, D., Reicheld, F. & Scheffer, P. (2002) Avoid the four pitfalls of CRM, *Harvard Business Review* 80(2): 101–109.

Rogers, E.M. (1995) *Diffusion of Innovations*, New York: Free Press.

Smith, B. (2003) The effectiveness of marketing strategy making processes in medical markets, PhD thesis, Cranfield School of Management.

Smith, W. (1956) Product differentiation and market segmentation as alternative marketing strategies, *Journal of Marketing* 21(July): 3–8.

Wilson, H., Daniel, E. & McDonald, M. (2002) Factors for success in relationship marketing, *Journal of Marketing Management* 18(1–2): 199–218.

Wind, Y. (1978) Issues and advances in segmentation research, *Journal of Marketing Research* 15: 317–37.

Yankelovitch, D. (2006) Rediscovering market segmentation, *Harvard Business Review* 84(6, Feb.): 122–31.

Chapter 3

INNOVATION

John Saunders
Distinguished Professor at AUDENCIA Nantes Ecole de Management

Veronica Wong
Professor of Marketing at the University of Sussex

John Saunders is Distinguished Professor at AUDENCIA Nantes Ecole De Management, Nantes (France). His major research interests are evolutionary marketing (the application of evolutionary theory to marketing), sustainable marketing and the future of marketing. Among his contributions to the academic community are the editorship of *The International Journal of Research in Marketing*, President of the European Marketing Academy, Dean of the Chartered Institute of Marketing and Executive Dean of Aston Business School.

Veronica Wong is Professor of Marketing at the University of Sussex and has also been a faculty member at Aston Business School, Loughborough University and Warwick University. She is a Research Professor at AUDENCIA Nantes Ecole De Management, Nantes (France) and Visiting Professor at the School of Business, Renmin University of China, Beijing (China). Her areas of specialism include New Product Development and Sustainable Marketing and she contributes to the activities of several international, academic and professional bodies. Positions held include the Presidency of EMAC, the European Marketing Academy, Fellow of the Chartered Institute of Marketing (CIM) and member of its Academic Senate.

Developing and launching new products has always presented vital challenges for marketers. Success does not only come from focusing on proven marketing techniques – it comes from fully integrating marketing into every aspect of the genesis, design and launch of a new product. This starts by developing an innovation culture throughout the organisation, encouraging everyone to share their research and insights, and working together to develop new products. Marketing occupies a pivotal position in product innovation. With a keen focus on the market, marketers are ideally placed to develop and deliver the products that customers want.

Lessons from the history of innovation

Business history is full of product innovations – some wildly successful and market making, some not. Interestingly, even when products were superior to others or offered significant advantages and benefits to customers, this was no guarantee of success. Business leaders and marketers, puzzled at the failure of what should have been a popular new product, often asked one simple question: What did we do wrong? To improve their approach, marketers needed to look closely at the reasons some new products succeeded while others failed. Given the enormous investments involved in developing new products, it remains vital for organisations to address this issue and get their approach right.

Key concept

Marketing and innovation

Marketers are essential for innovation, for example to advise on pricing and sales channels and execute marketing campaigns. Marketers' contributions are felt in a variety of ways and some of the most notable include:

continued on next page ...

- **Maintaining a clear focus on customers' needs.** To commercialise a new product, marketers have to help ensure that the organisation's research, strategy, processes and planning start and end with the customer.
- **Testing new products.** Technical flaws can be revealed by testing the product in the market before launch. This has been especially popular in the development of software products.
- **Analysing competitors.** Competitors may react aggressively to the launch of a new product. Marketers, aware of the precise nature of the competitors' threat, are well placed to take pre-emptive or retaliatory action.
- **Pricing.** Clearly, few issues are as significant at launch as product pricing. Just ask Lockheed, who overpriced the L1011 airplane and failed to compete with the McDonnell Douglas DC-10.
- **Predicting demand.** Over- or under-supply of a product can be disastrous, highlighted by the example of EMI Medical. Part of marketing's role is to prepare and predict demand accurately.
- **Carefully timing and executing the product launch.** The business needs to maintain an external orientation to make sure that the launch is timely and successful. Marketers also need to design the most effective 'go to market' strategy for the new product and successfully execute the campaign.
- **Coordinating the work of different departments.** Coordination is vital if a new product is to be developed and launched successfully. The one factor that unites everyone in the business is the customer, and an essential aspect of marketing is making sure that everyone in the business is coordinating their work and focusing on the customer.

It is often easy to see why a product progressed the way it did long after the event – that is the nature of hindsight. Yet it is necessary to look backwards in order to move forwards. Looking at the fortunes of others has highlighted the key factors we need to consider when dealing with product innovation. It is also the case that the success of some marketing campaigns led to the belief that marketing's reach needed to extend deeper into the organisation. Yet, while there are many aspects to the successful launch of a new product, there is one thing that particularly stands out: the offering must resonate with customers.

In the 1980s, Amstrad's PC2000 computer and Rover's Sterling car both suffered because of technical unreliability. While engineering design and manufacture may seem outside the domain of marketers, there are ways for marketing to support the research and development and the manufacturing sections of an organisation that might have helped both of these companies. For example, it is possible that technical flaws could be revealed by testing the product in the market before launch.

In the 1970s, despite being the pioneer of computerised tomography (CT) scanners, the British company EMI Medical failed to establish itself in the market. In part, this was because it had failed to anticipate the aggressive reaction of its competitors who had rapidly entered the market, taking advantage of EMI Medical's lack of capacity to deal with burgeoning demand. The lessons were clear: in-depth market research and analysis would have helped EMI Medical gear its production capacity to meet demand, while assessing competitors would have improved its marketing strategy. Anticipating how your competitors are likely to react enables you to circumvent any threat and to prepare your response ahead of time in an adaptable marketing strategy; forewarned is forearmed.

This is a good time to overturn the myth that excellent technology sells itself. It doesn't, as EMI Medical found out. People sell technology to people. This may seem an obvious point, but it is worth stating because it seems that some organisations have been so focused on the technology that the benefits of the product have blinded them to the single most important factor: the customer. To commercialise a new product successfully an organisation's research, strategy, processes and planning have to start and finish with the consumer.

Poor timing of a product's launch can result in spectacular failure. One example is so famous that the name of the

Marketing occupies a pivotal position in product innovation. With a keen focus on the market, it is ideally placed to drive, shape and develop the new products that customers want.

product has become synonymous with uselessness. In the late 1950s Ford introduced the Edsel car. Unfortunately, there was a downturn in the economy and people turned towards smaller, more fuel-efficient cars. Barely out of production, Ford found that the market for the Edsel had evaporated. Ford is not alone: there are many examples of companies that would have benefited from conducting thorough economic analysis. Changes in the performance of the economy (or changes in legislation) can signal imminent changes to consumption habits.

Business history is littered with cautionary tales highlighting the need for marketing to ensure success with new products. For example, Concorde overestimated demand for an airplane whose technological benefits were not valued enough, and Sony's Betamax video tapes were sidelined by competitors' VHS tapes. To be fair, analysing the reasons for some campaigns succeeding and others failing has revealed how easy it is for even well-planned campaigns to go wrong. Significantly, though, it is also clear that companies can fail to optimise the potential of a new product: they may have done quite well, but they could have done *much* better.

The pharmaceutical giant GlaxoSmithKlein showed what could be achieved when the skills and insight of marketers were brought to bear on product development, operational factors and market-entry strategies. The highly successful launch of Zantac (an anti-ulcer medication) followed detailed, thorough market research and planning that identified the market potential and informed every stage of the product's lifecycle. This success highlights the need for companies to examine how they are structured and how the different business functions work together.

Looking back, why some innovations catch on while others fall by the wayside can be puzzling. We all use the 'Qwerty' keyboard; we rarely question why we use it, we just do. Despite being easier to use, the alternative 'Dvorak' keyboard never caught on. Market rejection of superior products has been a loud wake-up call to marketers. Regardless of all the undoubted progress in techniques and strategy, we were clearly missing something quite fundamental. We needed to understand the essential nature of how ideas and innovations get adopted and diffuse through the market. This search has taken us on a root-and-branch investigation of market dynamics, psychological factors and human behaviour to arrive at a deeper understanding of customers.

The experience of innovation in organisations has shown that marketing cannot be viewed in isolation. It is essential that all aspects of a product's development, production and launch are fully integrated and operating efficiently – from inception and design to production and marketing. This requires:

- A coordinated, company-wide effort
- Clear communication
- Attention to detail
- A complete focus on the customer.

Any single aspect can undermine success, so it is important to be vigilant at every stage. We have learnt just how critical it is to conduct market research and industry analysis, to iron out any technical or operational issues and to analyse competitors, as well as getting pricing and the timing of the launch right – and we are still learning. The lessons for marketers from business history are insightful, but what are the rules today? Several issues are significant, starting with product innovation.

Product innovation at work

The challenge of innovating, and in particular marketing's role in this vital activity, is clearly the subject of a great deal of writing and research. In this chapter we focus on the essentials of two activities: product innovation and commercialisation (or taking the product to market).

A process for new product development

There is no question that our ability to market new products has greatly improved in recent years. One of the most useful methods for innovation marketing is the NPPD process – New Product Planning and Development. This process includes several specific stages covering all aspects of a product's development and commercialisation, greatly improving the product's market potential. These stages include:

- Business and marketing strategy
- Generating and evaluating ideas
- Analysing the business case
- Addressing development and production issues
- Testing the product
- Commercialisation.

In addition, research based on a comparative study of 50 new product successes and 50 failures introduced into the UK (Keegan, Davidson & Brown, 2005) suggests that successful new brands owe their success to three simple, obvious but highly compelling factors:

- A significant price/performance advantage over existing brands. In simple terms, the new product is better: either better value or capable of being sold at a premium price.
- A significant difference from existing brands. It is important to have a clear differential advantage or a unique attribute or set of attributes.
- First-mover advantage. Being first into the market, even with a slightly inferior product, can be decisive. This contrasts with followers who, without a clear advantage or superior performance, often struggle to gain market share.

The last point in particular is controversial and, clearly, there are significant risks with being a pioneer. The benefits, however, include the fact that news of an innovation is always greatest in the early stages; this offers maximum communica-

> There are three criteria for successful product innovation: better products with a sustainable differential advantage; a focus on customers, leading to a clear marketing orientation and a successfully executed marketing plan; and technical proficiency.

tion impact in the market. As a result, the pioneer brand can capitalise on consumer interest, for example with widespread consumer trialling leading to word-of-mouth communication and testimonials. Finally, to follow the pioneer, competitors have to improve their market position. In short, their products need to be better or cheaper to make the consumer switch.

Succeeding with strategy

A marketing strategy for a particular product must be part of the organisa-tion's overall business strategy. The strategy should start by understanding what your business is or what you want it to be. This will help you decide which products will help you achieve your goals. You should also consider your company's values and culture. Where you decide to position new prod-ucts in the market will depend on these issues. It is essential for marketers to be involved in the development of the company's overall strategy, as their insight and skills will help to identify the market opportunities and generate effective campaigns for new products that will be capable of achieving company goals and generating growth. Also, aligning marketing strategy closely with overall strategy improves the likelihood of a successful marketing campaign, as this will ensure that the messages and company brand are con-sistent for consumers and supported by all parts of the company – which is necessary for building and maintaining long-term customer relationships.

Your strategy and strategic direction will also be shaped by the company's resources, capacity and capabilities, including the possibility of forming stra-tegic partnerships with other companies. The type of new product you choose will depend on your objectives and resources, as each type is useful for dealing with different market situations – for example whether you are aggressively entering an existing market, trying to maintain your market share, asserting your technical leadership in the industry or wanting to generate growth without incurring high costs or risk. Developing a new product that does not match your business goals, resource levels and capacity is very risky and potentially ruinous.

Understanding the different types of new product

It is tempting to think that there are one or two categories of new product. In fact, part of the challenge facing firms is to choose the type of new product that is to be developed. There are six categories, including:

- Products that create an entirely new market, for example Sony developing a personal hi-fi, the Walkman.

- New product lines enabling a firm to enter an established market for the first time, for example UK retailer Marks & Spencer entering the home furnishings market.
- Adding to existing product lines, for example Apple adding the iPad to its existing range of computer products.
- Improving or revitalising existing products in a way that enhances performance, increases perceived value or replaces old products, for example UK bank Barclays becoming the word-leading supplier in the rapidly growing market for Exchange Traded Funds with its iShares service.
- Repositioning current products to target new customer segments or markets, for example many major sports and sporting clubs positioning themselves as family-friendly entertainment rather than simply a male-dominated activity.
- Cost reductions that provide existing or mature products at a lower cost, while delivering similar performance, for example Dell and other computer manufacturers offering the same laptops today as they did two years ago but with a significant price reduction.

Ensuring effective analysis

Getting innovation marketing right is a complex task requiring a deep understanding of a range of topics, including economic, technological, social, political and legislative developments, as well as knowing your industry and market. Clearly, a keen focus on your competitors is also essential. To assess customers' behaviour, you need to understand their entire environment – including psychological motivations, group dynamics, sociological factors and economic pressures. It is not enough to know any one of these or even a few, you have to know them all. Probably more so than in any other form of marketing, new products can fail by an oversight in only one small area. From economic forecasts to neuro-marketing, the array of expert knowledge that can be called on is huge, providing a vast amount of information for marketers to use.

Preparing your operations and procedures

Another important consideration is having processes and capabilities throughout your organisation that enable you to develop new products quickly, without compromising product quality or launch timing. This has the advantage of establishing your brand image as efficient as well as enabling a rapid response to changes in market conditions or customer preferences.

To achieve efficient operations, companies are increasingly using multi-disciplinary teams from all business functions working closely together. This reduces the time needed to take a product from inception to launch. Companies also need to streamline their decision-making processes to ensure an innova-tive approach – getting to market before your competitors means that speed and accuracy are essential. Significantly, generating popular new products will strengthen your position in the market, reducing the market share of competi-tors, even squeezing them out completely, and creating a significant barrier to entry for newcomers. It will also add long-term value for the organisation and brand.

In essence, firms that successfully prepare their operations and proce-dures and work continually to improve them are more competitive and leaner – ready to exploit market opportunities, enjoy first-mover advantage and dominate their industries.

Customer focus and testing

One significant reason new products fail is that they are not conceived, shaped or launched with enough focus on customers. It is imperative for companies to seek, value and respond to the opinions of customers before the product is fully launched. Of course, this is not always an easy task, because customers do not always share their views hon-estly or because they may find it difficult to predict their future

> Regardless of how impressive your people think the new product is, success is entirely about how the customer views the offer.

needs. Nonetheless, a new product that strays too far from the views and behaviour of its existing or potential customers, or fails to anticipate their response to the product, will not succeed.

There are a number of ways to develop an effective marketing plan, including:

- Initially testing customers' responses to the concept of the product (concept testing)
- Testing the actual product with customers (product-use testing)
- Limited distribution of the product to test the product in real buying conditions (market testing).

Testing gathers useful data that can be used to devise the best marketing strategy, gear up production and distribution, and allow for refinements to be made to the product to meet customer needs, thereby minimising the financial risk and maximising the market potential.

Testing also provides valuable insight that will help you to:

- Set the right price
- Know what messages you should convey and how to position the product
- Understand which customer segments to target
- Differentiate the product from your competitors' – as well as screening products early on to eliminate ideas that have limited market potential.

Also, by allowing some customers to use your product prior to a full launch, you can identify useful improvements, iron out any kinks, reveal how customers use the product in practice and even make a start on word-of-mouth advertising and raising market visibility.

In addition to the time involved, the main consideration of product-use testing and, in particular, market testing is the risk of alerting competitors to your product. Innovation

> While testing may be costly (particularly market testing), it is not as costly as launching a product that misses customers' expectations. The results of testing will ensure that you get your product offering right.

marketing has had to find ways around the various peculiarities that surround new products. For example, where finances, time or brand reputation are concerns, there is no reason you could not have a more limited market test – the costs are lower, the data would still be valuable and the exposure to publicity is less.

Avoiding the pitfalls of new product development

One of the great benefits of this process for new product development is that it helps avoid failure. The typical reasons for failure include:

- Inadequate market analysis, in particular failing to understand customers' reactions to new products, their specific needs and preferences and potential demand
- Technical difficulties with the product or service
- Underestimating competitors' reactions and strength
- Inadequate marketing activities and resources
- Unrealistic pricing
- Poor timing of the launch
- Production and supply problems.

These factors can appear in several different forms and we have identified six types of new product failure (Table 3.1), together with ways in which they can be overcome (further detailed discussion can be found in Wong, 1993).

Commercialising new products

Bringing a new product to market requires focus, commitment and, invariably, significant resources. It is worth noting that innovation does not simply mean developing exciting new products or product enhancements. It also means finding distinctive, compelling and memorable ways to attract and retain customers for new products.

Adoption and diffusion – the keys to success

Key to planning an effective marketing campaign for new products is to understand how products get adopted and then diffuse through the market. This knowledge is now an indispensable part of the marketer's toolkit.

First, you need to understand the dynamics of how products are adopted. This is decided by the interaction of the product's features and the behaviours

Table 3.1 Types of new product failure

Types of new product failure ...	... and how they can be avoided
The better mousetrap no one wanted Sometimes great firms produce great products that simply fail to sell. This often results from inadequate market analysis and a misunderstanding of customers' needs. This leads to over-estimating the number of potential users, poorly positioning the brand and inadequate product benefits.	The antidote is *clear market focus and insight*. This means generating insights through market research; clearly understanding customers' needs and wants; developing and applying segmentation, targeting and positioning skills; market testing the concept and the new product.
A 'me-too' product hitting a competitive brick wall Sometimes products simply fail to make an impression on the market. This is usually because they are not sufficiently innovative or different; they are poorly branded, positioned or marketed; or the company under-estimates competitors' strengths.	The solution is to apply all of the essentials of new product development. This includes generating creative ideas; conducting market research; improving marketing effectiveness; applying segmentation, targeting and positioning skills; anticipating competitors' responses; and, in particular, differentiating the product in a way that customers genuinely value.
Misplaced competitiveness and one-upmanship Sometimes an aggressive competitive response is to produce a new product – but one that is inadequate. The product fails because it may not be sufficiently different or innovative; the competitor's product (or its ability to keep customer loyalty) may be superior; or your marketing may simply be weaker.	In a competitive situation, the best approach is to pay careful attention to generating creative ideas; to monitor current and potential competitors carefully; and to prepare for retaliation. For long-term success, it is also important to develop a product improvement strategy and to develop and deepen marketing proficiency (including segmentation, targeting and positioning skills).

continued on next page ...

Environmental ignorance

This occurs when a firm fails to monitor or understand the changing nature of the market or customers' requirements. In this situation, a range of factors are either ignored or misunderstood (for example social, economic, technological, political, regulatory or cultural). This leads to weak or declining sales.

Again, the solution starts with clear and insightful market research. This involves regular market scanning and competitor analysis. Information and knowledge need to be widely shared and decision makers need to be close to the market.

The technical dog product

This occurs either when a product simply does not work as the customer expects, or when technical difficulties dog the customer.

The solution is clear: test the product with customers and end-users. And, of course, make a great product – this means investing in research, development and production.

The price crunch

An innovating firm may sometimes set too high a price for its new product, or competitors may take action (a price reduction or marketing campaign) that makes the new product look expensive and lacking in value (it is inadequate for the price).

In this situation the innovator needs to undertake careful market research to understand customers' views of pricing and market expectations; and create a better, more distinctive and high-value product to justify the price premium.

of different customer types. The factors that influence successful adoption and diffusion are typically:

- The advantages of your product over its rivals
- The extent to which your product matches current needs and customer behaviour
- Ease of use
- Overcoming customers' concerns through trial use of the product
- Being able to demonstrate the advantages of your product clearly to customers.

Targeting your customers

Marketing campaigns need to target the correct type of customer and there are five types: innovators; early adopters; early majority; late majority; and laggards. Your marketing plan should reflect the type of customers your new product is targeting.

For new products, it is often useful to target early adopters. This is because they are highly influential, able to persuade other customer types to follow their endorsements. Within the

> Your market research and testing will indicate where you need to position your brand. Essentially, this occupies a place that distinguishes you from your rivals and demonstrates the benefits of your product to customers. Brand positioning relies on an appreciation of the four Ps of marketing: product, price, promotion and place.

early adopters group is an even more-valued 'subgroup' to target: opinion leaders. Their influence is such that their endorsement of a new product can almost guarantee success, such as a respected film critic recommending a film. By targeting the early adopters (and innovators), you can create a ripple effect and then sit back and watch as the market embraces your product in ever-increasing circles.

To utilise the early adopters, a publicity campaign involving opinion leaders, including scientific experts and celebrities, can be useful. However, if there is no obvious famous individual, you can create your own 'celebrity' or 'expert'. This requires an advertising campaign that uses a figurehead, someone whom people associate with and believe that they can trust. You should also target appropriate magazines and associations to which early adopters are likely to subscribe. It is useful to look at your own sales records to identify customers who are interested in new product developments.

Marketing innovative new products requires a cross-company approach to strategy. The challenge of taking a new product to market is enormous, and the whole company needs to be geared accordingly. This starts with examining the company's fundamental set-up, procedures, values, culture and direction. For the marketing of innovative products to work, companies need their structure, communications, capabilities, resources, employee engagement and leadership to work together for a single focus: customers.

The future of innovation

Competition is fierce and consumers are increasingly well informed, with high expectations. The development of crowded global markets, distinctive competitors and connected customers means that differentiating your business and products is paramount. It is not only that companies need to produce new, improved products; they also need to understand what consumers want and predict what they will need, develop appropriate products and then persuade customers of the benefits. This requires all business functions to work together, with a total focus on customers.

> The importance of engaging early adopters for new products cannot be over-estimated: if you are not able to get them interested, your product is likely to wither on the vine.

An innovation culture

Innovation is a culture, not an act, and it should diffuse throughout the organisation. The future will lie with organisations that realise that

> Innovation is nothing without the ability to commercialise new products properly. Rather than the future belonging to companies that innovate, it really belongs to companies that have a culture of innovation.

marketing a new product is not an isolated activity that largely occurs long after a product's inception and development. Marketing should be fully integrated into the entire lifecycle of a product. As well as determining the correct timing, pricing and messages, market insight should be used at every stage – from generating original ideas for new products to informing design and production issues and marketing plans.

The future will undoubtedly pose many challenges and, to ensure success, marketers need better access to other business departments, including those once thought of as 'out of bounds', such as research and development. Marketing insights need to be rigorous, original, insightful, understood – and applied across the organisation. Although it has been said that the future belongs to companies that innovate, the truth is more complex: innovation is nothing without the ability to commercialise new products properly. Rather than the future belonging to companies that innovate, it really belongs to companies that have a culture of innovation.

Understanding the essentials of developing and commercialising new products is important, but one point should always be kept in mind: change is constant. So is there anything more or better we could do? The answer, almost certainly, is yes. Marketing is all about change and improvement. Essentially, it is a profession that values innovation.

Key questions about innovation

- Does your company have a culture of innovation?
- Are your innovations completely focused on customers?
- Which type of innovation (e.g. new product line, repositioning) is most relevant for your business?
- How is your product better than (or different from) competitors'? How do your processes compare with competitors' and customers' expectations?
- What customer need does the new product meet (or predict will be needed)?

continued on next page ...

- Is the new product easy for customers to understand and use?
- Do you change the product in response to market testing before launch?
- Can the product be seen by potential customers? Can they gather information and the opinions of other users whose opinions they respect?
- How much input does marketing have in product development and strategy?

References

Keegan, W., Davidson, H. & Brown, E.A. (2005) *Offensive Marketing: An Action Guide to Gaining the Offensive in Business*, London: Heinemann.

Wong, V. (1993) *Innovation: Identifying and Exploiting New Market Opportunities: A Handbook for Managers*, DTI, London: HMSO. Part of *Innovation: The Successful Exploitation of Ideas*, a series of handbooks written by Dr Veronica Wong for the UK Department of Trade and Industry (predecessor of Department of Business, Innovation and Skills).

Chapter 4

Philip Sheldrake
Founder and Partner of Influence Crowd LLP, Main Board Director of Intellect and Board Director of 6UK

Philip Sheldrake is an expert in marketing technology, digital marketing, process engineering and change management. He works with organisations to improve their sensitivity to their publics and to become more effective and efficient in their proactive and reactive interaction. He helps organisations sustain this advantage by identifying appropriate performance measures facilitated by the new marketing technologies, and integrating these into the organisation's business performance management scorecard. For further information, visit: www.influencecrowd.com

When we talk about digital, we're talking about the digits 0 and 1 – the simple, binary language of computers. Computers power the Internet and modern telecommunications, providing an infrastructure that delivers consumer content, conversations, applications and services. This, in turn, has attracted mass involvement and participation, which has led us to digital marketing and its language of persuasion.

Digital marketing encompasses a very wide range of platforms, media, channels, tools, services and applications. This chapter takes you on a whistle-stop tour of the past, present and future, highlighting some of the most significant, interesting or impactful developments.

The origins of digital marketing

Despite digital marketing's complex and dynamic landscape today, its beginnings in the 1990s were considerably more humble. As with many aspects of life, migrating from the analogue ('real') world into the digital realm meant that existing analogue concepts and practices were effectively transported over 'as is'. We moved mail over and called it email, for example. We went from having physical desktops, files and folders to, well, desktops, files and folders, and complemented our physical presence, our 'real' sites, with websites.

Early digital marketers should not, therefore, be criticised for being any less imaginative at their first attempt. Direct mail marketing was transported over to the digital world in the form of email marketing, while physical company and sales brochures were recreated online – albeit within the stylistic constraints of website design at the time. These were small steps for pioneering marketers, a giant leap for all marketing kind.

Such early forays made little or no attempt to use the advantages that digital possesses over its non-digital precursors, and it's not surprising that such websites subsequently earned the unflattering moniker of 'brochureware'. Understandably, the absence of sophisticated tools and the lack of widespread connectivity, subscribers, bandwidth and affordability frustrated and constrained early digital marketers.

So what is it about digital?

In the modern hubbub of mobile apps, social networks, interstitials, search engine marketing, digital outdoor, augmented reality, Twitter and internet TV, the essence of digital versus non-digital is often forgotten – or at least buried. It is worth reviewing the advantages that digital technologies deliver, as these advantages drive innovation and the continuing transition towards digital and away from analogue. For example, digital technologies facilitate:

- High-fidelity distribution that is low cost (e.g. CDs and memory sticks) or very low cost (by eliminating physical media altogether)
- Real-time, low-cost (or zero-cost), two-way transmission of information
- The potential to augment *broadcasting* (defined as communication with all endpoints simultaneously) with *unicasting* (communication with just one endpoint) and *multicasting* (communication with a group of endpoints)
- The potential to elicit instant responses at a known or zero cost to the responder
- The ability to satisfy inbound requests for information, almost instantly and through automated communications
- Implicit communication, which means learning about the recipient's regard for marketing delivery and potentially their regard for and use of the product or service – by monitoring actions, behaviour and public commentary
- Archiving communications for analysis, measurement and evaluation.

A range of digital marketing innovations have sprung from each of these characteristics. Indeed, reading the list can be a great way to translate the seemingly abstract language into more familiar digital marketing tactics. By keeping the characteristics expressed as generic as possible, you'll be able to go through the list again and think of alternative ideas and ways of working.

You've got mail

The growth of digital technology is fuelling an unprecedented explosion of marketing innovation. Indeed, it's difficult to recall the days when major milestone innovations were achieved only once or twice a decade. You need only have been online for a dozen or so years to recall the days when emails arrived so infrequently that a large internet service still thought its customers would like a vocal announcement of their arrival. Despite spam having pre-dated the first email marketing campaign (according to Wikipedia), consumer use of email has increased almost exponentially. For example, statistics, extrapolations and counting by Radicati Group from May 2009 estimate the number of emails sent per day (in 2009) to be around *247 billion*. This means that more than 2.8 million emails are sent every second, with spam account-ing for around 80 per cent of these messages. Significantly, genuine emails are sent by around 1.4 billion email users.

Yet we were using digital phone networks long before the internet arrived in most homes. According to *GSM World*, we were sending just 0.4 SMS messages per GSM customer per month in 1995, rising to 35 by 2000. The Mobile Data Association records August 2001 as the first month in which over a billion text messages were sent in the UK; by 2009, we were sending a billion text messages every 3 days and 17 hours on average, a rate of more than 3100 per second.

YouTube launched in May 2005. By the time of its second birthday it was consuming more internet capacity than the entire internet had in 2000. Over 24 hours of video footage was uploaded to YouTube for every single minute of May 2010, and it served 2000 million views a day. To put that in perspec-tive, that's double the volume served just seven months earlier, and nearly double the prime-time audience of all three major US broadcast networks combined.

Digital marketing at work

Digital marketing encompasses a wide and expanding range of topics and this chapter cannot do justice to the full scope, depth and speed of change of each specific technique. There are, however, six main themes that are particularly significant and need to be discussed further. These are:

- Websites and direct marketing
- Social networks and media

- Display advertising
- Mobile
- SEO/SEM
- Analytics.

Websites and direct marketing

Websites and direct marketing are both independent of a third party's media ownership. They are disintermediated, 'owned media' and are increasingly put to work in tandem.

Websites

Websites represent an incredible and unprecedented marketing opportunity. Unlike the analogue company or sales brochure, websites can be kept up to date, provide content that is multimedia and interactive, connect visitors to independent endorsers, and enable customers (and other stakeholders) to discuss your products, your support and the marketplace as a whole, both with you and with each other.

There are many facets to website strategy and design, but perhaps these can be grouped simply as:

- Getting people to the website
- Sparking and maintaining their interest once they're there
- Convincing the visitor that your product or service will satisfy their needs
- Getting them to buy your product or service (or equivalent objective).

The acronym AIDA describes this four-step process: Attention, Interest, Desire, Action.

Analysis of a website strategy's regard for each of these four steps betrays the strategy's maturity. At the amateur end of the spectrum, you have the 'build it and they will come' crowd who believe that a 'great' website will pull visitors in by itself. Now that the reality has disproved this belief time and time again, this mistake is repeated less often.

At the expert end of the spectrum, not only does website strategy include a series of tactics designed to drive visitors to the site, it is hyper-sensitive to one simple fact: there are millions of other places on the internet the visitor could zip off to in a mere click or two. Indeed, if visitors aren't reminded every few seconds why they are on your website, their departure may be considered to be the default action. It's for this reason that two fundamental website performance metrics are *bounce rate*, the proportion of visitors who don't go anywhere on your site beyond the page at which they arrived; and *exit rate*, a metric for each and every webpage, indicating how frequently that page loses visitors' interest to the point at which they leave the site.

The *click path*, the route a visitor takes around a website and their interaction with the site, may be an indication of the degree to which the website is piquing interest and desire for the company, product or service. Indeed, it might even show how frustrated users are in finding what they're looking for!

The best metric to use depends entirely on the action that you want the website to drive. Most obviously, a purchase is the ultimate outcome for an ecommerce website, but other actions may include registering contact details for a follow-up sales call (a 'callback'); leaving contact details and opting in to receive digital direct marketing communications; printing off directions to the high-street store; completing a customer or visitor survey; or emailing friends and associated social bookmarking and networking actions.

Website designers and developers do not have an easy time. They must:

- Recognise AIDA and understand how it will be manifest
- Adhere to accessibility legislation (the law governing the ease with which the website may be used by people with disabilities)
- Understand and work within complex technical constraints that change from year to year
- Recognise entrenched user expectations (e.g. a search facility goes top right, primary navigation goes along the top)
- Comply with an organisation's brand bible and strive to meet or exceed expectations for 'look and feel' for a number of key individuals (of course, many of these individuals may not be able to express their thoughts well, or even agree with one another at all!)

Perhaps website design and development constitute the most challenging of digital marketing tasks. Perhaps, given that it is such a specialist domain, it's the task where the gap between those who 'do' and those who commission remains greatest.

In conclusion, a website should never be for the website's sake, but needs to be closely designed and maintained to achieve previously agreed goals and performance metrics. These metrics should be designed to help achieve business outcomes rather than merely outputs such as clicks, unique visitor growth and page views.

Digital direct marketing

Digital direct marketing, for example via SMS or email, pushes the marketing message out, hopefully pricking the attention of the target and raising interest in the product's benefits. Like its analogue equivalent, digital direct marketing urges a response – the response rate being an important measure of the campaign's success and a metric more easily measured in the digital domain than the analogue.

Email (direct) marketing most often encourages a click through to a website and often a webpage dedicated to the campaign, known as a landing page. This is where the interest can be converted into desire and ultimately action. SMS marketing may aspire to do the same, particularly with the advent of smart phones that are capable of browsing the internet, often inviting a response via SMS to secure opt-in and to build engagement; or, via premium-priced services, to charge the respondent for digital content that is then dispatched by return (for example, this happens with the sale of ringtones).

Whereas SMS has non-negligible costs per message, the near-zero cost of email demanded legislation to dissuade the overly aggressive or less ethical marketer from bombarding targets with spam. Article 13 of the Privacy and Electronic Communications Directive in 2002 prohibits the use of direct digital communication for marketing purposes other than when the recipient has opted in (given permission) to receive the communication from a specified party for specified purposes. Communications relating to ongoing customer relationships are exempted, and various platform-dependent mechanisms ensure that any recipient can opt out at any time. The CAN-SPAM Act of 2003 is the US equivalent.

For such legal and associated technical reasons, a breed of specialist email marketing services has thrived. These specialists make it their business to ensure that your email avoids the spam filters and gets to the right recipient at the right time, in the most appropriate format, and with built-in campaign performance measurement capabilities. Often, an organisation will prefer outsourcing to these service providers rather than undertaking the task entirely in-house.

Social networks and media

The 1999 book *The Cluetrain Manifesto: The End of Business as Usual*, by Christopher Locke, Rick Levine, Doc Searls and David Weinberger (http://en.wikipedia.org/wiki/Cluetrain_Manifesto), asserts that the internet allows markets to revert to a bygone era. In fact, the internet transports us back to the days when a market was defined by people gathering and talking amongst themselves about a buyer's reputation, seller's reputation, product quality and prices. This was lost for a while as the scale of organisations and markets outstripped the facility for consumers to coalesce, but the consumers' conversation has now been reignited.

Of course, a change in market dynamics invokes changes in marketing.

Interestingly, Professor James Grunig, a noted PR theorist, saw this coming. His four models of public relations, published in the early 1980s, include the two-way symmetrical model described as using communication 'to negotiate with publics, resolve conflict, and promote mutual understanding and respect between the organization and its public(s)'. This focus on dialogue rather than monologue has proven to be a useful model for many marketing disciplines, not only PR, in adapting to the new market dynamics wrought by social media.

An example of a successful approach is provided by Harley-Davidson, which rarely approaches any marketing campaign (or indeed any product) without consideration of the one million-strong Harley-Davidson Owners Group. Indeed, why would any marketer wish to ignore such an evangelical fan base?

The marketing for almost every product and service lies somewhere along a spectrum from static brochureware to inspiring engagement and community. Modern marketers must get to grips with the views expressed via social media by advocates and detractors alike. They must understand the potential for helping to nurture

Marketers must get to grips with the views expressed via social media by advocates and detractors alike. They must improve their expertise in navigating this unpaid media.

the former and work with the latter, and they must improve their public relations expertise in navigating this unpaid media (also known, for very good reasons, as earned media). Only then can they hope to design marketing strategies that capitalise on the new market dynamic and avoid the new and plentiful pitfalls that it presents.

When we talk about marketing strategies, we're not talking of a 'Facebook strategy' or a 'Twitter strategy'. Facebook and Twitter happen to be the social media darlings at the time of writing. Indeed, given the decline of AOL, Friendster, Bebo and MySpace, who's to say what the future holds for these firms? The point is that rather than building your marketing strategy around individual platforms or services, it must be built out from a deep understanding of the character of social media. Services such as Facebook and Twitter are channels and may, therefore, require a suite of associated tactics to be deployed to accomplish the over-arching strategy. Moreover, with such a mature definition of your strategy, you'll be ready to move quickly and effectively should it help you prove that the 'next big thing', waving its shiny logo at you and your stakeholders, is indeed a perfect channel for you to continue to execute your strategy.

This approach also holds true for the time when movements such as Open Social (www.opensocial.org) result in social media participation more evenly across the biggest network of them all, the World Wide Web. Now that's something you need to be ready for. (Social marketing is discussed in depth in Chapter 12.)

Display advertising

In 2010, Yahoo! operated the world's largest display advertising network, with Microsoft a close second. Unsurprisingly, Google is also increasingly aggressive in this space. Yahoo! defines display advertising as 'graphical advertising

... that appears next to content on web pages, instant messenger applications, email, etc. These ads, often referred to as banners, come in standardized ad sizes and can include text, logos, pictures, or more recently, rich media.' A show reel of innovative ads on the Yahoo! network from 2009 can be seen on YouTube (http://bit.ly/yahooshowreel).

According to IAB Europe/Screen Digest (www.iabuk.net/en/1/europe sonlineadmarketcontinuestogrow020610.mxs), €4.55 billion was invested in display advertising in Europe in 2009, representing 30.9 per cent of online advertising spend. Despite its size and significance, display advertising has problems. For example, can you recall the last banner ad presented to you? No? Well, that's because mature Web users have learnt to tune out the locations of these ads in their visual scanning of Web pages. Can you recall the last display advert that obscured some of the page's content, or delayed your access to it, in an attempt to grab your attention? Yes? Well, perhaps you may also remember being annoyed; not exactly the positive emotional response any brand wants to elicit!

Intuitively, advertisements that interrupt cannot aspire to be as effective as those that your targets opt in to see or, indeed, actively seek out. One of the biggest success stories in recent times has been Cadbury's drumming gorilla, various recordings of which have been viewed over 10 million times on YouTube alone. The question here, of course, is whether the ad would have been so popular had Cadbury not interrupted TV viewers in the first place to show it. And is it an 'ad' or entertainment, or simply an entertaining ad?

Innovations such as the fast-forward facility of personal video recorders have left the 30-second ad format with an unclear future, but perhaps the 3-minute or 15-minute ad, or 'branded content', may be in the ascendant. If it entertains, if it provides useful information in a digestible format, if it answers questions or helps someone fix a pain in their lives, then you will have won their approval. And while the exact mechanics that determine whether a specific piece of content 'goes viral' (gets passed around and around) remain uncertain, much the same rules apply today as in 1962 when the first edition of Everett Rogers' seminal *Diffusion of Innovations* hit the bookstores. Analogue or digital, we're still human.

This is not the space for a rigorous analysis of the current state of digital advertising, however, so I'll cheat instead by directing you to a polemic published on TechCrunch by Eric K. Clemons, Professor of Operations and Information Management at The Wharton School of the University of Pennsylvania (http://tcrn.ch/advertfail). Here he asserts:

- There must be something other than advertising.
- Advertising will fail; not least because consumers do not trust it, consumers do not want to view it, and mostly consumers do not need it.
- Alternative models for monetisation are available.

You may not agree with his arguments and supporting material, but then it wouldn't be a polemic! (Advertising is discussed in depth in Chapter 8.)

Mobile: Digital on the move

Mobile phones are the most personal consumer electronic device. When we're going out, they rank right up there with our keys and our money. They become an extension of their owner and their loss is mourned, literally.

Smart phones are the most personal of all digital devices. They are so advanced from the early mobile telephones that the word 'phone' persists in name only for atavistic reasons. They are address book, diary, digital messenger, web browser, games machine, music player, video player, navigator, video and stills camera – and phone. They keep you connected with those who are far away and disengaged from strangers nearby.

So when a marketer wants to make a connection, what better platform than the one considered to be the most personal and emotional? And one that is always with its owner and knows its location?

Without listing every set of mobile marketing tactics, this appears to be the domain where permission marketing is most critical. Increased emotional attachment to the device increases emotional interaction with the 'stuff' that the phone's owner wants on it, and quite possibly the emotional reaction to stuff that they do not.

This is where we meet the fuzzy lines between *specific permission giving* (phone owner: 'Dear Nikon, do keep me posted about Nikon'), *general permission giving* (phone owner: 'Dear service provider, I'm interested in photography') and *behavioural targeting* (service provider: 'Hi, we're tracking what you've been doing and we think you're interested in photography'). Of course, this issue applies to all digital platforms and media.

Perhaps the most misunderstood aspect of mobile marketing, at least for those not involved in mobile marketing from month to month, is the vastly different level of complexity compared to the 'big screen' of PC-based web marketing.

Just two lines of operating system (Microsoft Windows and Apple OS) and four main lines of browser (Mozilla Firefox, Microsoft Internet Explorer, Apple Safari and Opera) dominate the 'big screen' world. Nearly all screens are big enough to render most websites without the need for horizontal scrolling. Excepting Microsoft's historic refusal to keep its browser in line with web standards, this all makes for a fairly homogeneous environment compared to mobile.

According to Gartner (www.gartner.com/it/page.jsp?id=1306513), the top six mobile operating systems by sales in 2009 were Symbian, Research In Motion, iPhone OS, Windows Mobile, Linux and Android. When calculating the total permutations, however, you need to multiply the number of operating systems by the number of different screen sizes, screen resolutions, colour capability, and browser availability and capability. Add to that, depending on your intentions, the data bandwidth available and the presence or absence of Adobe Flash player, accelerometers and location capability, and you're dealing with many thousands of permutations.

Apple's doctrine that one phone suits all, running counter as it does to this complexity, may well have contributed to the iPhone's allure and undoubted success. This apparent relative simplicity, combined with the capabilities and design of the iPhone generations, has rapidly accrued a relatively large ecosystem, including avid marketers. Nevertheless, marketers should, perhaps, pause for reflection.

With the fourth generation of iPhone now on sale, the iPhone accounts for just 4 per cent of EU5 (UK, France, Germany, Spain, Italy) market share in 2010 (www.comscore.com/Press_Events/Press_Releases/2010/6/ The_iPhone_Reality_in_Europe_Low_Overall_Penetration_Enormous_ Impact). One mobile marketing consultancy, on being asked to develop an iPhone app targeting the UK teenager in 2009, felt compelled to point out that iPhone penetration of this age group is much lower than adult age groups. And the most memorable case of 'iPhone-crazy' to date must be the March 2010 launch by the UK Government's employment minister of an iPhone app to access the Job Centre database (www.telegraph.co.uk/finance/personalfinance/7415996/New-iphone-application-for-the-unemployed-criticized.html). Why would you need an app when this database is accessible via any browser, and what exactly is the market penetration of one of the most expensive phones ever made among the unemployed?

Interesting mobile marketing innovations to track include augmented reality and other location-based innovations; mobile social relationship management; the integration of paid and earned media; in-game advertising; mobile search advertising; and mobile payment services.

Search engine optimisation and search engine marketing (SEO and SEM)

Google created search as we know it today by replacing the easily abused keyword-based search with the now famous PageRank™ algorithm. Fundamentally, Google wanted to return more relevant results to its users, and not ones where the webmaster had gamed things (for example by pasting a dictionary into a webpage). Its conclusion: What more independent and objective measure of relevance is there than the opinion of other webmasters and content

> Typically, 50 per cent of Google users click the first result presented to them, 12–22 per cent the second result, and 10–15 per cent the third result. This tapers quickly down to just 2–3 per cent for the tenth result.

editors? A link to a web page became a vote for it, and a link from a page with a high PageRank was worth more than a link from a page with a lower PageRank.

Search engine optimisation

Search engine optimisation aims to ensure that a particular website accrues more links to its pages (inbound links) and includes the most relevant words and phrases most often used by people likely to be searching for information in the field concerned, in order that search engines return its pages higher up in relevant search engine results.

Typically, around 50 per cent of Google users click the first result presented to them, 12–22 per cent the second result, and 10–15 per cent the third result (www.seo-scientist.com/google-ranking-ctr-click-distribution-over-serps .html). This tapers quickly down to just 2–3 per cent for the tenth result, and that's for one of the ten that actually made it to the first page of perhaps many thousands of results. So, given the considerable advantage that accrues for first position, considerable interest and money are showered on SEO, but not always the right kind of SEO activity. In simple terms, if you undertake the SEO techniques recommended by search engines, then this is known as white hat SEO. If you undertake techniques that the search engines frown on, then that is black hat SEO, and that is risky because, if you're caught, the website may be delisted entirely by one or more search engines. Also, web pages written primarily with SEO in mind may well disappoint the human reader, which of course is not the objective either. A good maxim for SEO, therefore, is simply to author great content for humans first and machines a close second.

Two of the most interesting trends affecting SEO are the personalisation of search results and real-time search. When the order of results and the inclusion of some results ahead of others depend on a user's history of searches and his or her personal network of friends, it becomes less concrete to identify the position of a web page in the search results for a given phrase. Moreover, when higher weighting is attributed to content that isn't yet more than a few hours or perhaps even minutes old, how can anyone talk about being 'number one'? This has led some pundits to coin a term for this new facet of SEO: social media optimisation (SMO). The Wikipedia page on SEO is a great resource for those wishing to find out more (http://en.wikipedia .org/wiki/Search_engine_optimization), as is SearchEngineWatch (http:// searchenginewatch.com).

Search engine marketing

Confusingly, some consider that SEM encompasses SEO, while others would exclude it. We'll proceed here to look at the advertising facet of SEM: paid search. Paid search is an example of pay-per-click (PPC) advertising. Rather than advertisers paying just to have an advert displayed, as with display advertising, payment is incurred only on the action of a click, the click representing a user being directed to a relevant web page. Unsurprisingly, marketers generally love this closer association of payment with action. As a result, IAB Europe/Screen Digest (www.iabuk.net/en/1/europesonlineadmarketcontinue stogrow020610.mxs) identifies paid search as the fastest-growing advertising format, with €6.73 billion invested in paid search in Europe in 2009, representing 45.8 per cent of online advertising spend.

Paid search was first manifested as the 'sponsored' results appearing around organic (unpaid) text-based search results, often to the right, above and below. Now, contextually relevant ads are being wrapped around any and all formats of search results, including maps and videos.

With Google being the market leader for search, maps and video (it owns YouTube), it has by far the largest share (75 per cent) of paid search spend (www.clickz.com/3640523). This dominance helped persuade the European Commission and the US Department of Justice, in February 2010, to approve the joint venture of the second- and third-placed providers of paid search, Yahoo! (18 per cent) and Microsoft (7 per cent). Under the terms of this venture, Microsoft will provide the algorithmic, organic and paid search services, and Yahoo! will manage the premium, human-sold campaigns across both their respective inventory for 10 years.

Analytics

Analytics is a statistical science that helps marketers listen, measure, evaluate, understand, improve and respond. In my opinion, a marketer who lacks sophisticated comprehension of analytics is no marketer.

Analytics spans every aspect, every platform, every strategy, plan and tactic of digital marketing. Clearly, this is a vital, significant and valuable feature of digital marketing. As highlighted earlier, an innate characteristic of digital is the ability to archive everything for subsequent or real-time analysis.

So, for example, we can record the links that visitors click on, the media they play and the time they invest on our websites. We know the time they take to open our emails and the links they follow. We can even identify the location of our consumers interacting with our mobile campaign, if they let us, and what people are saying about our brands and our competitors' brands online. In fact, the possibilities here are expanding so rapidly that it seems likely that this will remain a fast-developing area of digital marketing in the future. For now, it is useful to consider two types of analytics: analytics of stuff we control and those of stuff we don't.

> Analytics is central to marketing and this is actually facilitated by digital technology, which possesses an innate ability to archive everything for subsequent or real-time analysis.

Analytics that are under our control

Owned and paid media are under our control. We say what the campaigns do and say, and how and where they say it. With increasingly granular information from intermediaries such as ad networks, we have pretty good control over who sees it too. Often measures are relative rather than absolute. You can only gauge the open and click rate of your latest email marketing campaign as poor, expected or outstanding, for example, on comparison with your historical campaigns and benchmarking information in your sector, as available. (The work of the Web Analytics Association and the Interactive Advertising Bureau should be acknowledged, which, at the beginning of the twenty-first century, undertook to bring some uniformity of approach and a set of tightly defined and standardised terms in their respective fields.)

In 2010, perhaps the least well-understood dynamic or ramification of analytics outside the discipline's cognoscenti is its facility to feed directly into an optimisation engine, bypassing the human ad planner altogether. With so many permutations to be juggled and analysed in order to optimise campaign effectiveness, no human can begin to compete with software and services designed for the job.

Analytics that are of concern, but not directly under our control

If optimising our approach to owned and paid media is a complex task, then finding, tracking, listening to and responding to unpaid or earned media is even more challenging. To help, it is worth considering the Barcelona Principles, a foundation for the measurement and evaluation of unpaid media developed under the auspices of AMEC.

The seven Barcelona Principles (reproduced with the permission of AMEC, the International Association for the Measurement and Evaluation of Communication) were agreed by delegates at the second European Summit in Barcelona in June 2010, organised by AMEC and the Institute for Public Relations:

1 Importance of Goal Setting and Measurement
2 Measuring the Effect on Outcomes Is Preferred to Measuring Outputs
3 The Effect on Business Results Can and Should Be Measured Where Possible
4 Media Measurement Requires Quantity and Quality
5 AVEs (Advertising Value Equivalents) are not the Value of Public Relations
6 Social Media Can and Should be Measured
7 Transparency and Replicability are Paramount to Sound Measurement.

Some of these principles sound simple and basic, but the maturity of analytics of unpaid media roughly lag that for paid media by a dozen years, primarily because the social web (Web 2.0) lags behind Web 1.0.

Given the vast quantity of unpaid media and the number of mentions of international consumer brands, marketers and PR consultants have no choice but to embrace analytical software and services. More controversial is the expectation that software can accurately determine the sentiment (also known as tonality, particularly in the US) of social media contributions; many new kids on the block think it can. However, many of those who have been doing this a little longer and make it their business to compare computed sentiment with human assessment believe it cannot.

More pressingly, while the need has been identified, this field currently lacks the universal definitions it needs for debate to be meaningful and to allow technical comparisons.

What's next?

The future of digital marketing can be viewed on two fronts. There is going to be much more of the same, and there are going to be some radically new developments that emerge.

Much more of the same

Our society is becoming increasingly digital: more 'always-on' connections to homes; more bandwidth; more capable telecommunications protocols; more capable mobile devices; cheaper and therefore more accessible computers; better browsers; more social networking; more digital outdoor signage; more capable in-store technologies; more digital TV and radio – the list goes on.

By itself, 'more' is not a particularly interesting observation. The interest comes with marketers' increasing focus on tying the marketing and brand experience together across multiple channels, to the recipients' delight and to enhance the campaign's effectiveness. Multichannel campaigns and analytics provide opportunities to reach the target and opportunities to touch the target more than once across all the media they consume, passively and actively. Also, by inviting targets to move with you from one medium to another, with appropriate incentives, you can increase their engagement and the longer-term likelihood that you will have influenced their regard for your brand or objectives in the way you planned.

But perhaps there's clever and too clever.

By now, many readers will have seen display ads for items they have previously viewed on an unrelated website – as if by magic! Except that it's not magic, and many recipients of this targeted advertising do not feel that tingle of excitement from having witnessed a magic trick, but the tingle of concern that they've been watched, unannounced.

The fallout in 2008 over secret trials conducted by BT in the previous year of Phorm's behavioural targeting technology is now considered legendary. Depending on your point of view, it represents a pivotal moment in the design of digital marketing practices, or a pivotal moment in the approach to communicating such digital marketing practices – or, in reality, a little of both.

Many potential digital marketing innovations walk a fine line between changing our society's cultural norms and invoking a backlash when they are considered to have pushed the norms too far. This brings us to the new stuff, for which this fine line is ever present.

The new stuff

Digital marketing came a long way in the 'noughties' and the pace continues unabated. Indeed, quite possibly it's about to get faster. In the space we have here, we can consider just two of the underlying drivers: data and the meaning of data.

The rise and rise of data

Every one of us is going to be producing more data describing our use of digital products and services. This is what some refer to as our digital exhaust or digital footprint, and what I like to call digital detritus. Detritus is a biological word for discarded organic matter, such as leaf litter, which is then decomposed by microorganisms and reappropriated by animal and plant life. It is interestingly analogous to our regard for and treatment of the data that we're all shedding.

> Data will increasingly help marketers 'close the loop' for customers, potentially leading to enhanced loyalty. Data will also help customers test marketers' claims and debunk those shown up as false or exaggerated.

So, if we already produce digital detritus in our daily use of digital products and services, and we're all going to produce more, why didn't we refer to this in the 'much more of the same' section above?

Well, because when it comes to data we're working on a logarithmic scale – we're talking about hundreds and thousands of times more – which means it may well prove to have some new important mathematical properties (from a complexity system perspective) that are attractive to marketers, customer service and product development teams. Moreover, we don't actually do too much with the digital detritus today. It mostly resides in inaccessible log files, although the technology for collating the data is becoming increasingly achievable and affordable.

What does this mean in everyday terms? We collect the clickpath of visitors' interactions with our website today, but we can't yet access the data describing their use of most brown and white goods. We can invite customers to share their location data with us via their mobile phones, but we can't yet help them review their driving style (excepting Fiat's Ecodrive facility, www.fiat.co.uk/ecodrive) or use of public transport. We can encourage consumers to reap the anticipated advantages of greener products and services, but we can't identify the actual advantage they achieve and reflect it back at them. We can market a food product's expected role in a balanced diet, but not the specific role it plays in a particular household's diet.

Data will increasingly help marketers 'close the loop' for customers, potentially leading to enhanced loyalty. Data will also help customers test marketers' claims and debunk those shown up as false or exaggerated.

This perspective on digital detritus is closely related to the Internet of Things. This term is exactly what it says on the tin: a network of objects, or things, not typically connected to the network at present. This includes things such as central heating, cars, lighting, power distribution, temperature and other environmental sensors, clothes and even fast-moving consumer goods packaging. These innovations are playing out right now.

> The Internet of Things describes a network of objects, or things, not typically connected to the network at present. This includes things such as central heating, cars, lighting, power distribution, temperature and other environmental sensors, clothes and even fast-moving consumer goods packaging.

The marketing ramifications of such an Internet of Things are manifold, and here's a very quick example. Does Bosch Siemens market and sell dishwashers or a dishwashing service? With the potential to monitor every dishwashing machine remotely in real time, how might preventive maintenance benefits be designed and marketed? How does this transform the concept of a warranty, and how might such a redesign of the proposition lay new foundations for a lifetime relationship with the customer? Is every future marketing communication personalised (and I'm not just referring to the address field)?

Here's an example of the fine line we discussed earlier. Tiny objects known as RFID tags are embedded in clothes for supply chain management and optimisation. Two customers enter your store, and as the tags remain readable remotely, your systems determine that one is dressed in clothes from Primark, the other Prada. How does your in-store marketing respond, and what impact might this information have on your pricing strategy?

The meaning of data

If Web 1.0 describes the first generation of the web, one pivoting around documents and ecommerce, and Web 2.0 is about social community and (user-generated) content, then Web 3.0 revolves around the Web itself understanding the meaning of community participation and content.

Web 3.0 is the term most often applied to this idea of a semantic web (although you may see 'Web 3.0' applied in other contexts).

When you see the word 'orange' online, for example, the computers that underpin the pre-semantic web simply 'see' six alphanumeric characters in a row. They're also very good at spotting when the same six characters appear in a row elsewhere. Yet the semantic web describes a circumstance in which the web knows orange to be a colour, a fruit and a mobile telecommunications brand; but not only that, the semantic web knows which of these three meanings is intended in each and every instance, just as humans do.

Wikipedia is undergoing a semantic web transformation right now, an initiative known as dbpedia. The BBC and the UK government are already there with the bbc.co.uk and data.gov.uk websites respectively, as is Tesco with some of its websites. Tests show that Google has already tweaked its PageRank algorithms to boost the rankings of semantically marked-up content over equivalent non-semantic content, constituting one serious reason for marketers to understand what is going on here (http://mashable.com/2010/05/17/youtube-2-billion-views/).

Fascinating insight is achievable with today's social web analytics services (www.socialwebanalytics.com), particularly those that move beyond keyword analysis and try to overlay a semantic interpretation of the content they discover. Yet this overlay, typically dependent on algorithms developed from a field of computer science and linguistics known as natural language processing, does not achieve the analytical or computational power of a natively semantic Web. If you're excited by your social analytics service to date, all I can say is that we've only just scratched the surface, and 'getting more semantic' appears to be an inevitable trend.

We can bring this section on the meaning of data to an alluring conclusion by broadening out the sources of data under consideration. Social analytics, website analytics, CRM analytics, retail analytics and analytics related to the

Internet of Things are most often treated as silos. The first marketers to tie them together, to begin to connect the data records in each database relating to the same stakeholder, will have what I describe with just a little tongue in cheek as an 'Awesome Analytics Advantage', or Triple-A for short.

> Analytics relating to social media, websites, CRM, retail and analytics related to transactions on the Internet of Things are most often treated as silos. The first marketers to tie them together, to begin to connect the data records in each database relating to the same stakeholder, will have what I describe with just a little tongue in cheek as an 'Awesome Analytics Advantage', or Triple-A for short.

Will your organisation be Triple-A? Just as importantly, how will your analytics affect social norms? Will you impress your stakeholders by championing their 'right' to 'own' 'their' data? Will you risk scaring stakeholders with your Orwellian powers, or will you take this opportunity to champion new approaches to stakeholder relationships, such as vendor relationship management (http://cyber.law.harvard.edu/projectvrm)?

However you look at it, one unquestionable trend is increased complexity. Can you imagine studying 'brand chaos theory'? For the next few years, just knowing the right questions may well put you ahead of the pack.

Digital Marketing. Deceased 2010. RIP

With the innate advantages that digital has over non-digital, we're on the cusp of ceasing to make the distinction of 'digital marketing' and, instead, just beginning to talk about 'analogue marketing' in its minority role. And when all media is 'social', or at least has a social component, will we cease referring to 'social media' and simply drop our vernacular back to 'media'?

With such an incredibly bright future, digital marketing and social media are dead. Long live marketing and media.

Key questions about digital marketing

- Do your digital marketing activities complement your business strategy?
- How can you use technology to add value to your customer relationships?
- Can you improve your online commercial offering?
- Can you improve the way you use technology to connect with customers, deliver services or provide customised information?
- Are you capturing the right information, do you have the right analytics and are you using this information routinely to inform decisions? Could this be improved?
- Are the opportunities provided by digital marketing fully integrated into your business – everything from recruitment to product development?
- How well are your digital marketing activities supporting your branding, advertising and other marketing priorities?
- Are there ways in which digital activities can be used to reduce costs?

Chapter 5

SALES AND BUSINESS DEVELOPMENT

Beth Rogers
Principal Lecturer and Programme Manager, University of Portsmouth Business School

Beth Rogers is a leading thinker on the subject of sales management. She is a member of the CIM Academic Senate. Beth chaired the UK National Sales Board 2005-2009 and was instrumental in the launch of the National Occupational Standards for Sales. She is Programme Manager for the MA in Sales Management at Portsmouth Business School. She has extensive practical experience in both sales and marketing in the IT sector and consultancy, where she has worked with organisations from start-ups to major global corporations in a variety of industry sectors.

Selling, sometimes misunderstood and controversial, is never less than essential. Like so much in modern marketing it relies on a trusted, ethical approach, innovation and the capacity to build profitable long-term relationships based on a clear understanding of the customer. Given its importance, it is valuable to understand the changing character of selling as well as what makes a great sales manager.

The rise of selling

We should never forget that the Chartered Institute of Marketing was originally established in 1911 as the Sales Managers' Association by sales managers keen to improve the standing of their profession! The last 100 years have seen a significant change in the nature and importance of selling. Professional selling often did not receive the recognition or respect it deserved during the twentieth century, although this is now changing. In fact, selling connects a wide range of activities in an organisation. For that reason it is both strategic and tactical, and should be recognised as important by everyone from the chief executive to the most junior new recruit.

The history of selling helps explain its character and current challenges. In the nineteenth century, merchants would buy from factories to sell to retailers, sometimes on an agency basis, but usually independently. This had been happening for hundreds of years and selling was synonymous with being a merchant. Sellers worked for themselves and created their own selections of products to offer to their customers. Few manufacturers employed salespeople. This started to change with the development of industry and global trade, particularly during the first part of the twentieth century.

Between 1900 and 1950 industry consolidated, creating for the first time the professional salesperson: an employee committed to selling one company's product and brand, and being paid a salary with commission. This created new challenges for organisations in recruiting, training and developing salespeople as both company brand ambassadors and entrepreneurial revenue generators. It was during this period that practitioners and writers such as Dale Carnegie began sharing their expertise and writing the rules of professional selling.

Regulation, ethics and the rise of purchasing

The period from 1950 to the 1980s was marked by the increasing regulation of sales activities. This was designed to introduce rules to protect consumers' interests, overcome the concept of *caveat emptor* (buyer beware) and make sure that selling was ethical and fair. Examples of such regulation in the UK are the 1968 Trades Description Act and the 1974 Consumer Credit Act. Both of these assumed vulnerability on the part of the consumer. Also, regulation in financial services was increased during the 1980s.

Social changes, including higher expectations of corporate social responsibility from legislators and customers, resulted in regulation that changed and professionalised selling. Another force that has shaped the way that organisations sell is technology. In essence, opportunities for customers to buy (and for companies to sell) broaden and increase with advances in technology.

> Opportunities for customers to buy (and for companies to sell) broaden and increase with advances in technology.

From the 1980s onwards a clear distinction in selling skills emerged between *business-to-business* (B2B) and *business-to-consumer* (B2C) sales. Significantly, this was driven by the professionalisation of organisational buying. In 1980 a small minority of purchasing managers were professionally qualified, but by 2009 a large majority were Chartered Institute of Purchasing and Supply qualified, and an MSc in Supply Chain Management is now necessary for some advertised positions. Sourcing goods and services has become a strategic function, partly driven by the necessity of maximising the value received from suppliers in order to be globally competitive.

The rise in standards of purchasing in industry and the public sector, underpinned by comprehensive information systems, has required more comprehensive skills from sales professionals working in the business-to-business sector. The rise of the internet has also changed the nature of business-to-consumer transactions. For example, consumers are now able to discuss suppliers online, visit price-comparison websites and share examples of both good and (especially) bad sales practice. This has helped develop to improve selling standards in consumer markets.

Today, despite some theoretical speculation about marketing making sales irrelevant and web-based transactions taking over from personal contact, the sales profession is still growing, and the number of people who describe selling as part of their job is also growing. It is the quality of selling that is recognised by commercial organisations as being essential for business success. Increasingly, world-class companies have established 'academies' for professionals who focus on account management, business development and sales. Of course, this also means that sales management, often portrayed in films and on television as the art of shouting loudly, has to claim its strategic role in the organisation.

The cardinal rules of great sales management

Understand that selling is strategic and essential

For too much of the past 100 years, salespeople and sales managers have not been held in equal esteem with other professionals. The portrayal of salespeople in popular culture, from Willie Loman to Del Boy Trotter, has been stereotypical and rarely complimentary. It is important to acknowledge why this happens: when selling is done badly, it is ghastly. Governments have had to act against general and specific types of misrepresentation in consumer markets, and poor selling practice has been a factor in many high-profile corporate scandals. Unfortunately, some firms persist with inappropriate ways of pressurising their salespeople and their customers. However, there is a flip side to this coin. When selling is at its best, it is exciting, creative and generates value and growth for the supplier, the customer and the economy – something that differentiates the employers of great salespeople in an extremely positive way.

Because of the sheer size and scale of selling, there is plenty of room for differentiation. There are more salespeople than accountants and marketers, and selling takes place in all industries, countries and some public-sector organisations. With such a large number of people involved in selling, it is a challenge for legislators, professional bodies and companies to provide frameworks that enable the best sales behaviours. The way in which selling has been managed is also problematic. It has been stuck in an operational silo

---

Key concept

Messages for sales managers

- *Remember that strategy matters and affects sales.* Sales managers need to help shape strategic thinking at board level.
- *Think about resources.* Sales management is all about deploying limited resources effectively.
- *Use boundary spanning.* Sales management means showing empathy and collaborating across business divisions. Central to this is the ability to see things from different perspectives and adopt a questioning approach.
- *Coach your team.* Great sales performance means coaching and supporting the sales team. It doesn't just happen by going on calls with them.
- *Organise your time and prioritise.* It is easy to become engulfed by data management – too much information can easily soak up time and stifle creativity. The key is to find the right level of information and analysis that works for you, providing the right level of insight.
- *Aim high and learn.* The best sales managers (and leaders generally) are self-aware and keen to learn and develop their skills continuously. This has never been more important than today, during a period of rapid and significant change.

---

and a paradox: on the one hand, selling is so important that salespeople must keep their sole focus on 'getting the numbers'; on the other hand, it has been viewed as so mundane and operational that its role in strategy formulation has been limited. Perhaps one of the most exciting things about the current state of selling and sales management is the emerging understanding and recognition of its strategic role. Looking after revenue generation, the 'top line' on the profit-and-loss account, can make the 'bottom line' so much healthier too. Without a healthy revenue stream, companies go under. Because of this inescapable truth, companies are developing innovative, strategic approaches to creating sustainable sales growth.

This situation has several important implications for sales professionals. First, salespeople need to understand strategy in general: what it means, why it matters, as well as how it is formulated and executed. This is vital because it enables salespeople to contribute effectively to business strategy. Second, salespeople need to understand the strategic thinking and input of purchasers, recognising that companies' choice of suppliers is based on their objectives and assessment, and they have to 'know where they stand' with the purchasing decision maker. It also helps if sales managers have their own strategic tool for analysing business relationships. For example, the Relationship Development Box is a valuable tool for analysing relationships. This is a simple approach to mapping customer relationships and it helps the sales manager to classify the level of investment required. (Detailed information about the role of the sales manager and sales management techniques is contained in Rogers, 2007.) This links closely with the fact that if sales managers are going to coach their team members to impress board-level contacts in customers' organisations, understanding business strategy is vital.

Manage different categories of business relationships

One of the advantages of the Relationship Development Box is that it allows salespeople to understand customers' different, specific requirements, adopt the best approach and allocate resources efficiently. For example, relationships can be strategic, prospective, tactical, cooperative or unprofitable.

Customer relationships can be strategic, prospective, tactical or cooperative. Understanding the nature of each relationship is vital. It not only enables the supplier to create value for the customer, it also affects the approach and the level of investment required.

Manage strategic relationships (key account management)

This is where, on the basis of rational analysis, you believe that the customer has strategic value to your company and where the customer believes that you can add value to their business. It's important to note that relationship quality develops over time, as the supplier creates competitive value and the customer feels able to trust the supplier to deliver.

> Central to the challenge of sales and business development is boundary spanning. Boundary spanning means understanding the customer's needs in depth and how the capabilities of your company can be applied to them so that both gain competitive edge.

Boundary spanning

Strategic business relationships need to be developed by account managers (senior sales professionals) with the skill of *boundary spanning*. Boundary spanning simply means understanding the customer's needs in depth and how the capabilities of your company can be applied to them so that both gain competitive edge. Such thinking skills, involving awareness, empathy, integrity and creativity, are difficult to develop. Not surprisingly, employers perceive a skills gap for senior selling roles such as strategic account management.

Value creation

For a customer–supplier relationship to be strategic, there needs to be some specific value development for the customer. At the very least this means customising a product or service, but customers increasingly expect process integration across stock control, logistics and finance, and high levels of innovation in joint product development and co-marketing.

Such high-level investments carry risks for suppliers. Companies are well advised to be very selective about the number and types of customers that can be truly strategic. And,

> Sales cycles can be shortened by creating opportunities for strategic customers to provide positive word-of-mouth recommendations to prospects.

of course, relationships change over time. Dismantling a strategic relationship can be very public and potentially damaging – for example, affecting the supplier's share price.

Develop prospective relationships

Companies in the twenty-first century are rediscovering the importance of growing from within – organic growth – rather than growing by acquisition. This means taking on the challenge of converting prospects and new or occasional customers into regular or strategic ones. While it is usually true that it is easier to sell more to a current customer than to gain a new one, it is also important to note that attrition is inescapable: no retention strategy can keep 100 per cent of customers. This means that new customers must be found, and they must be convinced to try something from you and eventually to prefer you over their current supplier. That requires some considerable skill in targeting and relationship development, supported by a regular and sufficient budget. Sales cycles can be shortened by creating opportunities for strategic customers to provide positive word-of-mouth recommendations to prospects.

The key to succeeding with prospective customers is to be proactive. Often, generating leads is not the challenge: what matters is following up with the right prospective customers in the right way and at the right time. This is especially true with business-to-consumer markets, where timing and speed are critical, but it also applies in business-to-business markets. Developing prospective customer relationships requires sustained effort, careful opportunity evaluation and efficient process support.

Understand and succeed with tactical relationships

One of the cardinal rules of selling is the need to make it as easy as possible for the customer to buy. This applies at every level, especially with tactical relationships. These are usually one-dimensional: customers' needs are given, their requirements are evident, and the challenge for the supplier is simply to find the most cost-effective way of delivering. Tactical relationships can be satisfied with a range of low-touch options, such as working with distributors (or resellers) or selling via call centres and web portals.

Customers never complain about things happening too quickly – for this reason web-based business transactions are increasingly popular. They are not only instant and suitable for urgent orders, they also provide customers with a high degree of control. Clearly, tactical relationships are often (but not always) a source of opportunity, with the potential to develop further. It is important not to trap small, occasional customers in silos; analysis and understanding of tactical purchasers are important. Indeed, some researchers have drawn attention to the high profit potential of tactical business.

Manage cooperative relationships

Cooperative relationships are those where your customer values you as a supplier, but the customer's value to you is low or medium. A great example is one in which a supplier provides parts for customers' obsolete pieces of equipment. Customers are pleased that equipment can be kept working, but maintaining old technology is a non-strategic activity for the supplier. Customers who want high volumes, but at deep discounts, can also be in this category. For this reason, cooperative relationships are not always or necessarily friendly; cooperative relationships may also be essential yet dysfunctional relationships. You can't live with them, you can't live without them.

The challenge with cooperative relationships is to ensure that they are maintained with a modest level of investment. A focus on core performance such as price, quality and delivery is necessary, but standardisation and process cost reduction will be preferred to customisation. This requires a careful, analytical and questioning approach from the account manager.

Recognise and exit unprofitable relationships

Business relationships have a lifecycle. For example, 25 per cent of business relationships that are important to a supplier today will fail within a few years. Sales managers need to be masters of exit strategies. The ability to terminate in a constructive way those business relationships that are no longer mutually beneficial could be a competitive strength. It is useful to understand the causes of conflict and some of the reasons business relationships end. Key factors include a breakdown in communications, cost (or price) issues, a change in strategy, a collapse of the status quo (for example if a customer suffers a financial crisis), changes in the product or service offer, complacency, product problems, a critical incident or simply a change of personnel.

If a customer relationship is in crisis, there are several possible options, depending on the nature of the problem. These include working to avoid conflict and conflict resolution. The key is to avoid complacency, to work hard resolving and improving the situation and to be pragmatic, realistic and fair when it is time to negotiate an exit.

Recognise the qualities of great salespeople

Each type of business relationship needs a different sales approach, and companies concentrate their most accomplished relationship developers on strategic and prospective customers. Where do these professionals come from if there is a sales skills gap? Many salespeople see progression from a portfolio of small customers to high-potential accounts as a desirable career path, but equally account managers can transfer into sales from other functions – anything from engineering to finance. It is important for sales professionals to be sociable, but analytical and reflective thinking are just as important as communication skills in the modern world of complex solution selling.

The future: Twenty-first-century sales skills

Because of the current skills gap, recruiting, developing and compensating sales professionals is particularly important for the future of strategic selling. Four other challenges are also on the agenda of sales managers: reputation management, working with marketing, leadership and process management, including forecasting.

Managing corporate reputation

Following major corporate scandals in the first years of the twenty-first century, issues of accountability, ethics and public trust have become essential to manage for corporate survival, performance and success. Recent research suggests that a firm's reputation for social responsibility is more important to professional purchasers than any other aspect of the brand.

Given that salespeople are boundary spanners, balancing customers' expectations with those of their employers, they frequently encounter ethical uncertainty. They should know what situations cause problems and, crucially, they should know what to do to protect the company's reputation and their own. Legislation and compliance are often viewed as burdensome or threatening, when in fact they can be an opportunity to strengthen competitive positioning.

> Four challenges are shaping the future of professional selling: reputation management, working with marketing, leadership and process management, including forecasting.

The professionalism of salespeople – in particular, the levels of trust, respect and loyalty that they command – is a huge asset to the business. For example, a respected sales team can increase the value of the brand, build loyalty, deepen relationships, create new opportunities for the organisation or simply enable it to come through a crisis or period of uncertainty. A favourable reputation attracts shareholders and talented employees, as well as improving customer retention. Above all, a strong reputation is associated with superior financial returns.

The key to managing corporate reputation is, first, to avoid bad behaviour. This means rewarding salespeople fairly and consistently, avoiding the assumption of distrust and avoiding systems that may appear to be excessively controlling (this can result in retaliation). Of course, this guidance applies to any role in any organisation. A good salesperson possesses emotional intelligence and a conscientious approach. However, the sensitivity that this requires can easily lead to a feeling of pressure, particularly in the face of economic recession or downsizing.

The key is effective leadership and the ability to understand each individual team member: everything from the level of pressure needed for them to perform at their best (without becoming stressed) to their values and integrity. Other practical tools can also help, such as codes of conduct for giving and receiving gifts or for handling expenses. Make no mistake, ethics, integrity, trust and a commitment to the organisation's reputation – qualities that have always been important – are now essential for a successful career as a salesperson or as a sales manager.

Working with marketing

From the customer's perspective, sales and marketing are perceived as sharing responsibility for creating a positive

> The professionalism of salespeople – in particular, the levels of trust, respect and loyalty that they command – is a huge asset to the business.

image of the company and communicating its value. In practice, however, sales and marketing are usually separate departments, with tradition dictating that marketing is responsible for demand generation while sales is responsible for converting leads into revenue. In practice, there is often friction and misunderstanding between the two teams. This was never an efficient or sustainable way to run a business. In the twenty-first century, with heightened global competition and a rapid pace of change, this friction is potentially toxic.

The benefits of mutual support between sales and marketing are compelling and include:

- *Collaboration*, with information sharing and people working collectively for common goals. This has a positive effect on business performance and directly contributes to a better working atmosphere, improved customer service and more opportunities for innovation.
- *Branding*, recognising that customers take into account a range of intangible factors when they are reviewing potential suppliers. For example, buyers need to consider the company, and its personnel, as trustworthy and even likeable. They value the prestige or other benefits provided by the brand, they want the message to appeal to them and be consistent, and they need to know that buying from the company is a sound, reliable decision. These intangibles require sales and marketing to work in a mutually supportive way. Or, to put it another way, these intangibles and the firm's brand can be undermined by disagreements.

Several simple measures can help ensure that sales and marketing get along and drive the business's success:

- Clearly defining the roles and responsibilities of sales and marketing.
- Managing interactions and alignment. This includes managing meetings, sharing information, providing feedback, creating opportunities for

informal interaction and, in particular, establishing a routine way of working together.

- Collaborating in a way that goes beyond interaction. This involves shared processes, shared goals, shared values, mutual understanding and teamwork.
- Providing strong senior management leadership. This is where the direction and drive come from for a collaborative and mutually supportive relationship between sales and marketing.

The five tools of sales leadership

One of the challenges of managing salespeople is that they are typically independently minded. This can mean that they are driven and highly effective at developing great one-to-one relationships, but they are not naturally in tune with followership. This can make them especially hard to lead. Conventionally, leaders set goals, show the way forward, help to remove obstacles and enable their team members to succeed. This is vital for sales managers and account managers in charge of cross-functional teams, but several other aspects are also important.

The five tools of sales leadership are awareness, framework setting, extensive communication, coaching and development, and trumpeting.

Awareness

This includes self-awareness as well as an awareness of others. Crucially, the ability to motivate oneself and others starts with considered thought and reflection. Self-awareness and understanding are vital for learning, developing and being confident and focused. Leaders need to be able to understand how influential they are and their impact on others. Being aware of what motivates other people – their strengths, weaknesses and preferences – underpins the ability to build rapport and trust.

Framework setting

Leaders in any situation or context needs to be able to provide their team with a framework (or strategy) for achieving their objectives. This framework should include the expected outcome and, ideally, an example of what 'good' would look like. As well as setting the direction, it is also important for leaders to:

- Act as a role model and set high standards.
- Take personal responsibility; this both provides a role model for team members and means that the leader takes responsibility for the team's mistakes. This generates trust and support and helps to encourage strong performance.
- Set appropriate standards for work and be a team player.
- Be a careful and active listener.
- Understand that they should never ask someone to do something that they would not do themselves.

Extensive communication

Communication is vital in every organisation and team, especially communication with salespeople. Information and understanding are needed for them to feel confident and simply to enable them to do their job. Communication includes active listening and questioning; the priority is to build understanding. The characteristics of effective communicators include:

- Clarity, openness and empathy
- Decisiveness and the ability to follow when necessary and take the lead as required
- The ability to build strong links at all levels of the organisation – from the top team to the receptionist
- Seeking direct feedback from customers and business partners
- Making what we say interesting as well as informative, through examples
- The ability to convey essential messages, including what the idea is, why it is important and how it can be successfully applied.

Coaching and development

Given that the context in which sales professionals operate is continually changing, with new, surprising and different challenges arising all the time, the ability to coach and develop people is an essential leadership skill. Kolb's learning cycle is an especially useful technique. It outlines a simple but effective cycle where *experience* is followed by *reflection, forming new ideas* and *experimentation* before returning to experience again.

In order to improve performance, salespeople require answers to basic questions including: Where am I going? Where am I now? How do I get there? How will I know when I succeed? Am I on the right track? Sales managers could just tell the salesperson their opinions about the answers, but coaching skills enable sales managers to help salespeople to work them out for themselves, which is more effective. Coaching succeeds by encouraging reflection and reinforcement and it is highly personal, enabling the individual being coached to overcome personal barriers or concerns.

Trumpeting

Feedback is a valuable gift and if someone has done something well (and with salespeople, success is usually obvious), the first thing to do is to congratulate and thank them. This can include specific rewards, both symbolic and financial.

Managing and improving sales processes

All successful sales organisations have efficient and excellent sales processes. Several issues are important:

> Managing and improving sales processes is not a one-time activity. Sales processes require continuous attention and improvement.

- Making sure that sales processes comply with formal requirements and informal expectations
- Understanding if and why sales processes are failing
- Working continually to improve and develop sales processes

Improving processes is a constant challenge and, while each process may require a slightly different approach, there are several techniques that apply to all processes. First, *understand why change is needed*, what the business case is. In particular, how will it make things easier or more productive? Next, *set clear objectives and key performance indicators.* You need to know in advance the expected results and benefits, so that you know whether success has been achieved (or not). For example, the benefits of a shorter sales process might include a shorter sales cycle, reduced sales costs, reduced administration or greater customer satisfaction.

Key concept

Sales processes

What are the processes that need to be managed efficiently? Typically, they include the following activities. It may be useful to consider which of these processes could be improved within your organisation.

- *Information management* includes sharing information and market knowledge; managing customer and contact information; managing information about product, price, promotion and new opportunities.
- *Business management* typically includes planning and forecasting; budgeting; strategy formulation; and managing risk.
- *People management,* in particular managing performance (including motivation, evaluation, recognition and reward); recruitment; training and development; and disciplinary procedures.
- *Customer communications* includes processes such as customer demand planning; account planning; communications protocols; post-sales support; customer satisfaction surveys; as well as complaints handling and problem solving.
- *Process management* includes quality management and continuous improvement; managing change; corporate governance and legal compliance procedures.

Managing and improving sales processes is not a one-time activity. Sales processes require continuous attention and improvement.

The next step is to *assess or audit the current process.* You need to understand clearly and objectively what is wrong with the current process and why it is failing. Only then is it possible to *engage in process redesign.* As a general rule, it is wise to consult with the people who will be affected by the process change: what would they like to see? The next stage is to *consider any potential risks*; these may be strategic, reputational, operational, compliance, environmental, financial or related to information or intellectual property. It is important to align technology, undertake training, evaluate the effectiveness of the new process, provide a communications plan and seek feedback.

Managing and improving sales processes is not a one-time activity. Sales processes require continuous attention and improvement. The most critical process is sales forecasting, which can affect so much of the overall effectiveness of the organisation, as it feeds into production planning and cash-flow management. A sales manager should be persistently looking for ways to make the sales forecast more accurate, which often depends on other sales processes feeding into it and how progress through sales cycles is monitored and measured.

A final thought

Selling has come a long way in 100 years. From being viewed with occasional disdain or distrust, it is now seen as a highly skilled role and integral to other aspects of the business, such as innovation or brand building. One of the primary functions of senior managers is to lead the company's sales efforts and that means involving sales managers and salespeople in strategy formulation. The forces of technology, ethics and globalisation that are shaping other areas of marketing are also affecting selling, and will make selling more complex and sophisticated in the future. Sales skills and sales management skills therefore require considerable attention in company planning.

The 2008 Labour Market Information report in the UK identified that there is already a large skills gap in selling. The reasons this has arisen are twofold: first, people move out of selling because it is seen as a transient job; second, because of a lack of investment in training and development for sales professionals. Those problems need to be addressed by organisations, together with the education sector. Promoting selling as a desirable and enjoyable career is a twenty-first-century opportunity for individuals in sales roles, but also for organisations, government and society.

Key questions for sales and business development

- Do you understand the principles of business strategy: yours and your customers'? Can you see the big picture?
- Are you distinguishing between different types of business relationship and managing each one appropriately?
- Are you allocating the right resources in the right place, at the right time?
- Do you have empathy, and are you succeeding at boundary spanning – able to view a situation from the customer's perspective?
- How are you creating value for strategic customers? How could this improve?
- Are you proactively developing prospective relationships?
- Have you made it as easy as possible for the customer to buy?
- Do you have the right approach to managing tactical relationships?
- Do you recognise and know how to handle difficult, dysfunctional or unprofitable relationships?
- Are you managing your corporate reputation? Are your sales channels in tune with your reputation?
- How well do your sales and marketing professionals work together? Are they mutually supportive? What more could be done to develop this pivotal relationship?
- Do sales professionals have a voice at the highest level of the organisation? Do they help to formulate and execute strategy?
- Do the company's processes support professional selling? Are they efficient and consistent with the company's key sales messages?
- How strong is the leadership of the sales team? Can you recognise the qualities of great sales professionals? Are your salespeople given opportunities to learn, to develop their skills and to increase their experience?

References and further information

Kim, C.W. & Maubourgne, R. (1997) Value innovation: The strategic logic of high growth, *Harvard Business Review*, Jan/Feb: 103–12.

Kotler, P., Rackham, N. & Krishnaswamy, S. (2006) Ending the war between sales and marketing, *Harvard Business Review*, Jul/Aug: 68–78.

Rogers, B. (2007) *Rethinking Sales Management: A Strategic Guide for Practitioners*, Chichester: John Wiley & Sons Ltd.

Woodburn, D. & McDonald, M. (1999) *Key Account Management*, Amsterdam: Elsevier.

Chapter 6

CUSTOMER RELATIONSHIP MANAGEMENT

Merlin Stone

Professor of Marketing, Bristol Business School and Fellow of the Chartered Institute of Marketing

Merlin Stone is a leading author and advisor on Customer Relationship Management. He is Professor of Marketing at Bristol Business School and Visiting Professor at De Montfort, Oxford Brookes and Portsmouth Universities. He is also Research Director at WCL and a Director of Nowell Stone Ltd and The Database Group. He has authored many articles and thirty books on customer management. He is a Fellow of the Chartered Institute of Marketing and an Honorary Life Fellow of the UK's Institute of Direct Marketing. He is also on the editorial advisory boards of several academic journals and writes for several trade publications.

The value of CRM lies in its ability to help businesses improve their understanding of their customers. Organisations that do this effectively are more competitive and profitable, because they are better able to segment and appeal to different customers, develop and maintain profitable customer relationships, decide how to handle unprofitable customers and customise their offer and promotional efforts.

Vital, practical, insightful: Customer relationship management

Customer relationship management (CRM) is, quite simply, how companies manage customer relationships. Despite a straightforward goal, success requires sophisticated technology and analytical skills. By enabling organisations to focus on how they interact with customers, CRM enhances the customer experience and builds long-term customer value.

Unfortunately, there is often misunderstanding and a lack of consensus about the meaning of customer relationship management (CRM). This matters, because a narrow or confused definition can often contribute to the failure of CRM projects, with organisations either viewing CRM from a limited technology perspective or else undertaking CRM in a fragmented way. In truth, CRM systems are simply a technology-based tool for developing and using knowledge about customers. It is by developing and then improving their knowledge of customers that a firm's customer relationships (and the loyalty of its customers) are more likely to improve.

The growth of CRM

CRM emerged in the 1980s as a way of dealing with business-to-business and business-to-consumer relationships. It developed for two reasons: as a way of managing existing customers more efficiently and to gain new customers successfully.

The rapid growth of technology since the 1980s has led to much more customer information being available than ever before, derived through more contact with customers through call centres, direct mail, emails and the internet. This increased contact can be used to ensure greater understanding of customers' shifting preferences as well as providing an opportunity to sell.

> CRM means creating and using knowledge about customers. This knowledge is valuable because it enables the organisation to enhance its relationships with its customers.

CRM's popularity rose sharply in the 1990s, as organisations realised the need to become more customer oriented. The benefits are obvious: maintaining long-term customer loyalty ensures current cash flow and long-term stability. CRM has also increased rapidly in popularity because it is seen as a way of streamlining sales and marketing processes, improving sales productivity, generating cross-selling and up-selling opportunities, improving customer service, increasing the efficiency of call centres, enabling salespeople to 'close', improve profiling and targeting, reducing sales expenses, increasing market share, aiding new product development and contributing to higher overall profitability.

During the 1990s and 2000s businesses rushed to purchase CRM systems, while journals published numerous academic articles on the subject. According to research from Gartner published in 2008, the worldwide CRM market continued to grow for a fifth consecutive year. The Gartner report *Dataquest Insight: CRM Software Market Share Analysis, Worldwide 2008* estimated that the overall CRM market grew by 12.5 per cent in 2008, from revenues of $8.13 billion in 2007 to $9.15 billion in 2008 (this followed the even stronger growth rate of 23 per cent in 2007). (For further information see 'CRM Market Grows for Fifth Straight Year' on www.destinationcrm.com/.) Clearly, this investment would not have been made if CRM did not deliver bottom-line results. Significantly, the cost of retaining customers has been conservatively estimated at one fifth of the cost of acquiring a new customer. Therefore, existing customers generate bigger margins and better profit per customer than new ones, representing a significant return on investments in CRM.

CRM and relationship marketing

CRM is valued as the key to developing profitable, long-term relationships with customers that enhance a firm's competitive advantage. Fundamental to this goal is relationship marketing, which aims to move customers along a 'marketing strategy continuum'. This view was an important development in the growth of CRM and it led to organisations thinking in terms of selling to customers within an ongoing relationship rather than as a series of unrelated purchases (Ravald & Gronroos, 1996). It also brought the advantage of assuring customers who were making purchases involving high levels of perceived risk or service benefits.

As organisations have grown, building relationships with customers based on personal contact has become harder. While powerful user-friendly databases and improved telecommunications allowed large organisations to know more about their customers and competitors, maintaining effective contact with customers became harder. Personal contact lies at the heart of relationship marketing, so companies faced considerable challenges to find ways to overcome this problem. This situation has been further complicated by intensifying competition, with products and services no longer enough to secure competitive advantage.

The notion of 'total relationship marketing' came about to describe internal marketing relationships between managers and employees and between those in different functional areas. Both relationship marketing (RM), with its external orientation, and total relationship marketing, with its internal orientation, were incorporated into CRM. This heralded the change in business focus from customer acquisition to customer development, retention and loyalty.

One of the main aims of CRM has been locking in high-value customers through a process that identifies customers, serves their needs sensibly, uses customer information tactically and overcomes customer dissatisfaction. To achieve this, CRM started to focus as much on the emotional experience as on rational customer satisfaction. Interestingly, some organisations have encouraged customers to form their own communities and communicate with each other. All this customer collaboration has meant major changes to business models, with technology becoming a major enabler and anthropology and psychology expertise providing analysis and policy perspectives.

In order to fulfil its promise and potential, CRM strategy has become a key issue for many organisations. One of the main challenges in achieving this goal is improving the working of networks within an organisation. By this I mean that different departments and teams need to be able to work together, sharing their data and analysis, in order to deliver value and a quality experience to customers, improve processes, manage costs and, consequently, increase profitability.

From its early straightforward approach, CRM has grown in breadth and depth, requiring the insights of a variety of experts as well as company-wide interactions and collaboration. Looking at how CRM is currently working will offer important insights for the future. We can learn from the past and should not be deterred from implementing a successful CRM strategy. Besides, it is precisely because it is difficult that it has such potential. After all, if CRM were easy it would not enjoy the benefit of competitive differentiation.

Current thinking about CRM

Organisations know that it is essential for customer information to be current and usable, and they spend large sums of money gathering and storing customer profiles. However, all this information is of little real value unless it is manipulated and turned into useful, accessible information. New technology has enabled large-scale and efficient data warehousing that is capable of integrating operational and customer data quickly and effectively. Data mining can extract and analyse specific information from large amounts of data. This information is used to target customers across the world, to manage costs and supply chains and to ensure that goods and services are made available to the right customers, at the right time, at the right price. The key to success is often process management: integrating traditional functions (from enterprise resource planning and production to sales and personnel functions) so that the organisation's technological capabilities can meet its strategic and operational objectives.

Why things go wrong and what can be done about it

CRM is a common-sense activity with its origins in straightforward ideas of direct marketing, sales management, customer service and quality. Treated as a management idea, developing slowly and applied consistently over many years, it usually brings good results. However, if it is approached as a short-term fad it normally fails. By adapting and managing a broad range of network activities, communications, customer care approaches and other processes, CRM adds value, reduces waste and improves long-term success. However, when the technology fails to deliver the promised results or when an organisation has not adapted to meet customer expectations, CRM can became synonymous with failure.

Several measures are important to make sure that a CRM system succeeds:

- Ensure that your senior executives have ownership and leadership of the system.
- Build a CRM culture throughout the organisation.
- Educate everyone about how CRM delivers value – and train them in how the system works.
- Plan and monitor the implementation of the CRM system.
- Keep your main focus on understanding customers and what they want, rather than just looking at the technology – the technology is the tool not the goal.

The key to long-term customer value: Building the customer experience

To achieve the benefits of CRM, organisations need to change old attitudes, systems and procedures at all levels. Interactions and integration between different departments are crucial to successful CRM.

One approach that is particularly useful is Gartner's Eight Building Blocks of CRM. This outlines what organisations need to do to develop successful customer management (www.GartnerG2.com). First, the vision should set the agenda for the strategy and, crucially, for what type of customer experience is expected. The vision encompasses issues of leadership, market position and value proposition. This vision informs the CRM strategy, which includes clearly identified objectives and market segments as well as interaction and collaboration between departments.

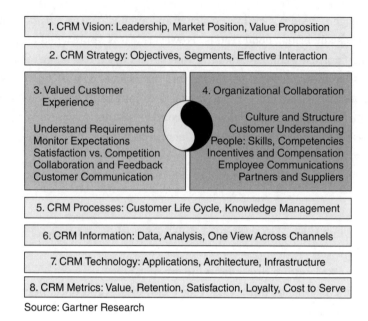

Source: Gartner Research

Figure 6.1 Gartner Building Blocks model

To succeed with CRM, therefore, organisations need to start by setting the vision and strategic context within which CRM will operate. Defining customers (their relationships and value) is essential. By identifying and analysing current and potential customers, it is possible to assess customer profitability. For example, many organisations find that 20 per cent of their customers generate 150 per cent of their profit, while some customers are unprofitable. (In the example in Figure 6.1, the unprofitable 80 per cent of customers generate a loss.)

The next step is to decide what kind of relationship you want with your customers – whether it should be more or less personal. Having identified and analysed these issues, the next challenge is to create the agenda for change and decide how the business will move to this new, improved position. Customers or customer segments must appear in the processes and not merely be submerged within sales territories. By this I mean that marketing, sales and service processes must be clearly defined for each kind of customer relationship. These will range from intense key account-type relationships, for very valuable customers, to near-automated processes, for the large number of less lucrative but still valued customers. The choice of supporting software then follows; crucially, software must be in the service of business objectives, never vice versa.

A customer-focused enterprise also needs suitable metrics. It is important to use metrics to understand customer segments and major individual customers, rather than territory or product line. To achieve the goals of a CRM system, a professionally managed programme of change must reach the whole company. This needs to explain the reasons for the changes and exactly how it will be achieved. A focus on relationships won't work on its own. In fact, there won't be a focus on relationships at all unless people believe in the change.

Are we getting value from CRM?

Businesses often ask what value they are getting from their CRM systems. This is not an easy calculation, because each activity has many stakeholders with particular ideas about value. Actions that add value for some may cut value for others. Also, each activity is closely interrelated, so it is hard to identify exactly which activity it is that is adding the most value. To complicate this further, the various business disciplines (such as operations and customer management) have been hijacked by software suppliers, so that the terms we use seem to apply to the software, instead of the management discipline that it supports.

Many attributes contribute to a compelling, attractive value proposition for the customer, and each of these attributes is obviously costly. So, to ensure a profitable return on your investment it is important to exceed expectations in the areas that really matter to each customer, while simply meeting expectations for the rest. Relationship management research techniques not only identify those parts of the customer value proposition and experience that each individual customer values most, but also *when* they want them.

The best way to build customer value and profitability is to identify and acquire potentially valuable customers, and then to invest in developing that potential by managing the customer experience and improving the relationship. This is achieved with a combination of product, service and the feel-good factor generated in many ways, for example by being visually appealing, using an appropriate tone of voice and attending to details at all the customer touch points (such as salespeople, call-centre agents, advertising, receptionists, product brochures and websites). The way in which the relationship develops depends on customers' expectations, and these arise from your brand promotion, word-of-mouth communication and reputation, past experience with the company and previous experience of other companies. Significantly, it is not necessarily the customer's experience of your direct competitors that matters, but their buying experience in general.

The moment of truth: Designing the customer experience

There are several major steps to take when designing the customer experience. First, find out which elements of your brand and image are actually valued by customers and are seen as different from competitors. Then use strategic relationship management research to determine how customers feel about the experience: what they expect and value. Using a combination of touch-point analysis, process mapping of customer lifecycle interactions and known relationship determinants, it is then possible to map out the *moments of truth* (MOTs) in customer interactions. This will reveal where the experience makes the most positive or negative impact on customers.

> To ensure a return on investment, it is important to exceed expectations in the areas that really matter to each customer, while simply meeting expectations for the rest. Relationship management research not only identifies those parts of the customer value proposition and experience that each individual customer values most, but also when they want them.

Next, establish the gap between desired and actual customer experience at each MOT. At the same time, you should understand employees' experience of these moments and compare this with the customers' experience. Your findings should then inform the development of new customer and employee experiences. Crucial to this is the ability to recruit, train, coach and provide incentives to employees that will support the new customer experience. In particular, your CRM strategy should help provide the experience needed by employees to offer a winning value proposition to each customer segment.

When trying to improve the customer experience, it is easy to assume that you know and understand your customers. This confidence is invariably flawed and incorrect. A new discipline of customer insight that merges market research and customer database analysis helps to overcome this. Many large companies have now appointed specialist customer insight managers and teams, and these provide a vital building block for successful CRM programmes.

The role and impact of outsourcing

Outsourcing continues to grow worldwide, with companies placing work with external partners that can provide the required expertise at the most competitive price. Manufacturers, for example, often produce their products overseas, where lower labour costs, economies of scale and access to global markets far outweigh the advantage of manufacturing at home. Also, the trend in outsourcing to call centres abroad is increasingly popular. While the advantages of outsourcing can be substantial, the possibility of adverse customer reactions should be carefully considered. For example, any negative aspects such as publicity about the working conditions of the local labour force or customers' concerns about a perceived loss of quality and privacy should be considered.

UIA Insurance is a business providing insurance to the not-for-profit sector. Its business philosophy is anchored on socially responsible principles towards its members, customers, staff, partners and the community. This organisation decided that it would be better to keep its customer care centre in house for several reasons. These included the ability to deliver prompt, effective communications and feedback between departments,

> CRM involves a network of relationships within the organisation and it must work closely with marketing. To maximise the gains from CRM, organisations need to make sure that their managerial and marketing expertise, data and information technology, business networks and processes all work together.

to monitor service quality, to resolve customer queries quickly and to enable better linkage across all the business functions. UIA felt that its brand reputation for good customer care would be supported by avoiding outsourcing.

Significant business reengineering is imminent due to the nature of changing global markets and shifting social, economic and political influences. To devise a successful strategy that captures and retains customers within this changing business environment, organisations need to invest heavily in CRM. The future of customer relationship management is exciting, precisely because the market is facing difficult and changing times, as it will equip organisations to take advantage of the many opportunities that still lie ahead.

Managing the financial aspects of CRM

The growth of CRM has not been without its problems. Major investments in CRM systems are valuable but complex activities requiring expertise, commitment, foresight and attention to detail. For example, a multichannel strategy requires an in-depth appreciation of the ramifications of how investment in one channel affects the success of another. Also, customer privacy and security issues pose problems, while new regulations emerge regularly that affect CRM strategy. All of these issues hinder the difficult task of accurately identifying the profitability of different customers.

In addition, CRM investments are expensive not only in monetary terms but also in the management time required for implementation. If the wrong system or strategy is chosen, if there are any technological failures in a CRM system or poor management support from CRM providers, the resulting loss of working capacity can have a devastating effect on the profitability of customers.

Given the levels of investment required, implementing a CRM system often requires a compelling, persuasive case. Proponents have to persuade others of their arguments and this is not always easy, especially as realising a return on investment in CRM often takes longer to appear than the next quarter (or even the current financial year). This problem is compounded by managers focusing on short-term goals, as their performance and advancement are assessed by short-term successes. Without incentives, managers can lack the motivation to deliver CRM goals. In this case, it is unlikely that customers will benefit. So, incentivising your people is crucial to realising the potential of CRM.

Another difficulty in persuading colleagues to invest in CRM is the unavoidable argument that there has been little strong evidence that customers actually want to be managed in a relationship. In addition, many large corporations have used their relationships with suppliers to extract maximum value for their operations while returning minimum value to customers (www.GartnerG2.com), further increasing scepticism. These issues have clearly hurt the case for CRM. However, it is important for organisations to look deeper into their customer relationships. If customers do not want to be managed overtly, this may suggest that your CRM needs to be more sophisticated in its approach and that the relationship itself needs to be more intelligent. Customers may take elements of the relationship – such as receiving exactly what they want, when they want it – for granted, not even viewing it as a relationship (which for some people may have the uncomfortable implication that their privacy is being invaded). Moreover, the potential of negative publicity (such as not passing on savings to customers or using methods that are environmentally unfriendly) should act as an argument for managing your customer relationships more carefully.

A model for CRM

A useful model for CRM is the Essential Navigator® (Figure 6.2). This was developed by Customer Essential Ltd as a result of extensive experience of successful customer management delivery over 25 years with leading organisations worldwide, in both business-to-business and business-to-consumer environments, and through academic work with partners and universities (www.customeressential.com).

This model is a realistic set of best practices in customer management implementation. It is being continuously reviewed and new best-practice inputs provided into the base.

The northern part of the model covers Data and more structured deliverables in Customer Management. The southern part covers Customers and more community and environmental activity; the eastern is focused on People

Figure 6.2 The Essential Navigator

and more introspective and organisational aspects; and finally the western is about Business and more financially and benefits-related deliverables.

Customer Essential uses the Navigator tool to support organisations that are trying to make progress in one or more of the following areas:

- Building an ideal customer management model.
- Identifying the current status of customer management and comparing this with known best practices.
- Raising and gaining agreement on strategic changes required in the approach to customers.
- Identifying smaller-priority deliverables to tackle quickly.

The methodology looks for areas of best practice in each of the model segments, which are summarised below.

Business

- Developing a prioritised implementation approach for successful customer management.
- Customer targeting and selection process prioritised by value.
- Plan for customer management with intended targets and objectives, by appropriate segment or business line.
- A customer proposition that actively reflects the different customer priorities, e.g. through contractual terms, pricing mechanisms, product development path, service interventions, use of technology, payment terms.

Customer

- Plan for customer experience based on segment and value.
- Customer research is carried out on a regular basis. The research carried out enables update of the proposition and delivery process.
- Customers can easily provide feedback or complaints through whichever means they choose. Their feedback is acted on and an update is provided.

Data

- The core data required to plan and manage customers is in place. The right permissions and quality are managed on this data, to which a value is attached.
- The data used to drive customer management is captured and managed to ensure maximum quality (recency, completeness).
- The systems and data environment in place ensure that those dealing with customers on a regular basis have access to the crucial data required.

People

- The organisation prioritises, measures, recognises and rewards customer management from initial acquisition through to retention.
- The spirit of the organisation reflects a passion for customers.
- The leadership team prioritises, drives, mentors and coaches successful customer management in line with business priority.

- The core competencies to understand, plan for, prioritise and manage customers are in place.
- The appropriate organisation structure is in place to enable the successful focus on and delivery of customer management.

The challenge of implementing CRM

There are several significant reasons many organisations fail to excel with CRM. For example, businesses understand that future success relies on their customers' satisfaction in the present, as well as the related concept that acquiring customers is usually much more expensive than keeping them (on average, it costs five times more to recruit a new customer than it does to keep an existing one). However, they fail to respond and invest the resources that are needed to ensure customer satisfaction. Managers continually challenge the fact that markets need investment; service levels need to be sustained, despite their cost and the shifting economic cycle; and a balance needs to be struck between retaining existing customers and acquiring new ones. Often, the problem is not misunderstanding what needs to be done, it is actually doing it.

The other simple truth confronting many companies is that customer care invariably incurs immediate or short-term costs, while some of the financial benefits may only emerge in the medium to long term. While quantified objectives can be set that can translate directly into turnover or bottom-line profits, managers are continually facing the question: 'Can costs be significantly cut by reducing the trappings of extra service?' The answer, of course, is yes, the costs of customer service can always be cut. This extra cash can then benefit the rest of the marketing mix, for example by allowing prices to

> Customer acquisition is an expensive process, while customer retention boosts sales, profits and return on investment. There is, therefore, an opportunity to carve out a competitive advantage through CRM programmes if they are carefully planned and executed.

be cut or extra spending on promotion or product improvements. On the other hand, would a lack of service create a competitive disadvantage? Or, put another way, would extra service create competitive advantage, and for how long?

These challenges can be partly addressed by using accounting techniques to explain the benefits of CRM. This highlights the cost of acquiring customers, changes in the number of customers and changes in what each customer is buying, and it provides a compelling financial case for investment in CRM. In fact, it can be argued (Payne & Frow, 2006) that successful implementation of a CRM programme depends on four critical factors:

- *CRM readiness assessment* is an audit that helps managers to assess their overall position in terms of readiness to progress with CRM implementation. It also helps to identify how well developed their organisation is in the area of CRM, relative to other companies.
- *CRM change management* means achieving the organisational and cultural changes needed to succeed with CRM. Senior-level understanding, sponsorship, leadership and cross-functional integration are clearly critical in a complex CRM implementation.
- *CRM project management* requires cross-functional teams of specialists who manage the enterprise's CRM implementation programme. Successful CRM projects deliver their CRM objectives. These are derived from the corporate objectives and support the overall business strategy.
- *Employee engagement* means gaining active support and commitment from employees for CRM projects. Companies are coming to realise that they cannot develop and operate customer-focused CRM systems without motivated and trained employees.

A central theme of most studies of success or failure in systems development and implementation is whether the project slipped badly, so that it was completed much later than the original deadlines. However, in our experience, CRM systems are different in that they usually support a large change in how a company works with its customers. This change involves learning by the company's staff, its system suppliers and consultants, the company's business partners (for example marketing communications agencies, call-centre suppliers, fulfilment houses) and, in particular, its customers. Learning and continuous improvement enable the company to create a new way of working with its customers, sometimes even creating a new or stronger relationship.

Customer relationship management has been one of the fastest-growing businesses and most energetically debated topics among business practitioners and academics. Companies continue investing huge amounts to implement CRM strategies and to develop the necessary tools and infrastructure. However, complexity and scale both affect the time it takes to develop and roll out a CRM system. 'Big-bang' approaches – large-scale projects with high levels of functionality – are not uncommon. However, although this approach might seem risky, the likelihood of success can be greatly enhanced by being clear and prescriptive. For example, a company that wants to dramatically improve both the quality and scope of its customer database and the quality of its interaction with customers does not have to invest in using new data through a new customer interaction system. Some or all of the new data can be used to enhance existing customer interactions. So, although we know that with information technology projects, project risk increases with project size, the risk can be reduced by having several interlocking projects and paying attention to developing a 'Plan B' to deploy whatever has been successfully developed, even if there are slips in other parts of the programme.

Many companies reduce the inherent risk of CRM by staging the introduction of key elements of the system so that the benefits are delivered early. They then continue to develop the system based on their experience of deployment. This also reduces the political risk of CRM programmes. For this reason, many suppliers of CRM systems and consultancy have created CRM programme planning and deployment methodologies that support accelerated early-development stages. At the heart of such methodologies must be a strong CRM programme planning methodology, one that is understood by senior managers as being the central focus of their governance for their CRM improvement efforts.

Those companies that think hard about the options for phasing and developing their CRM programme and consider them as related aspects of the same task are more likely to get the CRM systems they want.

The risk of a 'big-bang' approach is that all the requirements are gathered at the beginning of the project and applied in one continuous development period, before 'waterfall' testing and deployment take place. The waterfall model is a sequential process for developing software, in which development flows steadily, like a series of small waterfalls, through the requirements of analysis, design, development and integration, testing, implementation and maintenance. Although there are many arguments about the pros and cons of this model, it seems that large-scale projects that use this approach tend to have a high

> While CRM has made enormous progress and has benefited companies and customers alike, there is still much more to do – new challenges await and solving them will bring even more opportunity in the future.

risk of failure, to take longer to deliver benefits and to be less adaptable to continuous learning. As a result, the development effort invested in some functions may be wasted.

The waterfall model is associated with another systems development idea – 'big design up front', in which system design is agreed early on in the project so that the systems development effort can focus consistently on the required design. Of course, there is no perfect model for systems development. In fact, the waterfall method is often criticised because in the real world requirements do change, as systems frequently need design changes before their development is finished. Because of this, it is usually not possible to have smooth, step-by-step progress from design to implementation. Instead an iterative approach often proves much more effective at delivering business value in stages and reducing programme risk. Those companies that think hard about the options for phasing and developing their CRM programme, and consider them as related aspects of the same task, are more likely to get the CRM systems they want.

The future of customer relationship management

The continuing importance of CRM can be seen in how customers' experience of call centres affects profitability. Simply differentiating from competitors through a few separate features, such as price and product quality, is no longer enough. Increasingly, companies have realised that they need to compete with their rivals by offering a better customer experience at every level in which their organisation interacts with customers. The total customer experience will inform business strategy in the future, as this is where customer loyalty is won or lost.

There is a huge disconnect between how well companies perceive they are doing and how customers rate their experience. For example, using research from Bain & Company's customer survey of 362 companies, Meyer and Schwager (2007) revealed that while 80 per cent of the companies believed that they provide a superior service, only 8 per cent of customers felt that they received a superior service. Customers expect more and better, and if you don't provide these another company will. This has arisen because organisations do not fully understand what providing a superior total customer experience means and what it involves. To bridge this gap between customers' expectations and what they receive, companies need to use CRM more effectively.

CRM is concerned with managing the customer experience. So companies need to understand their marketing and ask customers what the most important considerations are for each experience that they have with the company. Asking questions about how well a company is doing for them, what it can improve and what competitors can do better, are all steps in the right direction. Getting the answers is helping to put the CRM system in order. Unfortunately, many experts believe that CRM has not delivered either the promised return on investment or more satisfied customers. Although this is beyond the immediate realm of many marketing communications managers, they need to understand and influence CRM systems. They also need to be aware that many companies are going backwards rather than forwards in improving levels of customer satisfaction.

> In the long term, customer service is not simply about customer care or product quality. It is about serving customers and finding distinctive ways to sustain a competitive edge. This also requires clear communications with customers so that they are fully aware, at all times, of just how good the company is, how much it tries, how it succeeds and how much it cares.

In recent years the global economic recession has destabilised the marketer's world by forcing many customers to change how they spend their money. Increasingly, many suppliers will have to adopt new tactics to retain their customers. After years of boom in which many companies found it easy to achieve steady growth in sales and customers, they are now facing a new, unfamiliar reality.

So, how are companies managing customer retention during the recession? My research has shown that many companies are not equipped to manage customer retention effectively, especially given the impact the financial crisis will have on customer spending. It is clear that while some organisations have implemented real-time customer-lifecycle management, early warning systems, price elasticity models and deal calculators, many are still failing to use the information and technology available in a sophisticated or effective way.

During these difficult, recessionary times, my research has revealed that external data is occasionally used for high-level modelling, with one or two companies employing it for detailed scoring, while two utilities used it comprehensively for attrition modelling. Credit score data was utilised, primarily to determine whether a customer should be retained. One financial services company used data on whether a customer had accessed aggregator sites as an indicator of possible attrition. The respondent that was a member of the Nectar loyalty scheme employed its data intensively for attrition modelling and prediction.

The use of real-time marketing was rare, the two exceptions being a telecoms company and a media company, with utility companies having plans in this area. This is surprising. Real-time marketing produces great results in terms of up-sell, cross-sell, retention and customer satisfaction. It also reduces costs in other areas, typically the batch marketing areas such as direct mail and outbound telemarketing. For most respondents, the recession had caused customers to search for more value, but generally not to switch more.

Clearly, in a time of sudden and deep recession, companies face significant challenges. Addressing these challenges means drastically improving their customer management techniques and processes. The recession looks likely to continue for some time, which means that companies need to deal with the inevitable surge in competition by developing a strategy for successfully managing customer retention.

A key weapon in improving marketing effectiveness in a recession is to optimise customer communications, both across different channels and over time. Real-time marketing that uses a 'next best actions' tool is ideal for encouraging customers to achieve their value objectives. This allows companies to discover which propositions work best for particular customers. It highlights the fact that there is only one way to realise this future potential: invest in analysis, systems and processes. Business success will be sustained if the organisation works to align its culture, structure, goals, strategies, policies, processes and customer proposition with what its stakeholders, business partners and suppliers want.

Key questions about CRM

- How do people in your organisation view CRM? Are they positive about it and do they understand its purpose and potential?
- Is CRM an integral part of your business processes?
- What are the problem areas for CRM in your company or department?
- Do the organisation's processes support your CRM strategy?
- Do you work with all the departments in your organisation to set your CRM priorities and to ensure that your CRM strategy is implemented?
- How do you use CRM in your marketing plans and priorities?
- What do you do to enhance the customer experience? How can this be improved?
- Are there aspects of how your organisation is managed or its business strategy that need to change for you to succeed with CRM?
- Do your customers always receive a consistent experience?
- If you outsource some of your services to third parties, how do you make sure that your brand, company's reputation and customer relationship policy are followed by the external organisations?
- If you are considering outsourcing, have you identified the potential risks to CRM?
- How will your brand be affected by outsourcing?

References and further information

Meyer, C. & Schwager, A. (2007) Understanding customer experience, *Harvard Business Review*, Feb: 117–26.

Payne, A. & Frow, P. (2006) Customer relationship management: From strategy to implementation, *Journal of Marketing Management*, 22(1–2): 135–68.

Ravald, A. & Gronroos, C. (1996) The value concept and relationship marketing, *European Journal of Marketing*, 30(2): 19–30.

Chapter 7

BRANDING

Graham Hales
Managing Director, Interbrand UK

Graham Hales is a leading authority on brands and branding. He is currently Managing Director of Interbrand UK, the world's largest branding consultancy. He has helped numerous leading global organisations to successfully develop and leverage their brands.

A brand is a living business asset, brought to life across all touch points, which, if properly managed, creates identification, differentia-tion and value.

Brands matter because they raise awareness of a product or service. They show what is distinctive about the brand and convey emotional relevance, making the case for purchases against other alternatives. This ability to influence choice can lead to price premiums, loyalty and advocacy that will create revenue and profit for the owner. This builds brand and shareholder value.

The rise and rise of branding

Branding has always been an issue of political, financial and social impor-tance. By considering the development and attributes of some of the world's most valuable brands, we can learn lessons on the challenges faced by all brands. During the last 100 years the evolution of branding has been invari-ably exciting, valuable, increasingly significant and, at times, a hotly debated topic, because brands often display the metaphorical signals of what a society values at a given moment in time.

Early approaches to brand management were simple, reflecting the immaturity of the discipline and the nature of the products. Initially, the modern concept of the brand manager originated in the days of fast-moving consumer goods – from Coca Cola to soap – when brand marketing was essentially about straightforward consumer products. With the growing com-plexity of markets and with so many markets now involving an element of service, branding and its experience for customers developed during the last decades of the twentieth century to become a much more sophisticated and involved process, requiring input from many parts of the organisation. During the development of branding one vital truth has increased steadily in understanding and acceptance: that branding requires everyone in the enterprise to understand what the brand stands for – its core purpose and reason for being – and then work in a way that genuinely delivers this to the customer.

How branding developed during the twentieth century

At first branding simply acted as a mark of ownership, the very term having emanated from permanently marking livestock to distinguish one farmer's property from another's. As commerce grew, people's commercial ambitions for their produce extended. Pretty soon brands started to compete with one another. Though techniques were haphazard, the forefathers of branding laid the foundations of what today has become known as a competitive claim: shelf standout and packaging identity. The industrial revolution gave birth to corporations, meaning that marks of ownership needed to extend across increasingly diverse entities. And as organisations grew, so did the breadth of the people they needed to connect with: customers, employees, prospective employees, suppliers and shareholders all needed to be influenced. With the increased complexity of organisations, the need to be more strategic in communications became evident. Complex messages had to be built cumulatively and consistently and with this impetus brand management was born.

If anyone had told you in 1995 that an internet-based business with no shops would become one of the world's biggest retailers and one of the world's most valuable brands, I doubt you would have believed them. Yet Amazon is now a household name, enjoying incredible success as a front-of-mind, convenient retailer. It has done this by understanding the customer, of course, but it also built on this understanding and applied its knowledge of customers to create a strong brand experience. Amazon remembers who you are, it 'talks' to you in a distinctive tone of voice, makes suggestions like a returning friend and is reliable in its fulfilment; rather more than your average physical retailer. This highlights the vital truth about brands: they are not simply a logo that is 'grafted on' to a business in a way that is superficial or skin deep, *they are the business.*

Brands and retailing

The power of branding is perhaps greatest and clearest in the area of retailing. At a retail conference that took place in 2009, two of the major awards for successful retailing were given to Apple. This generated a few mutterings among traditionalists that Apple was not a 'proper' retailer. This is interesting in view of the definition of retailing as 'the sale of goods in relatively small quantities to the public'. Unfortunately for many electrical retailers, Apple has not sold its goods in relatively small quantities. Also, what has made Apple rebrand the retail sector so successfully is the distinctive experience it offers customers. It has designed its stores differently to traditional retail outlets, offering its customers a different experience in line with its 'think different' brand. It also has a strong element of service integrated into its approach to retailing, rather than simply selling products at brashly discounted prices. The result of this different, branded retail experience is clear: Apple's average sales per square foot of retail space are $4032. This is a figure that compares very favourably with another successful electrical retailer, Best Buy, which averages sales of $930 per square foot.

Another example of a retailer successfully integrating brand management with retail is Tesco, the UK's largest retailer (and one of the biggest in the world). In its 'core purpose' there is a clear emphasis on service and creating value for customers:

> Our core purpose is to create value for customers to earn their lifetime loyalty.
>
> Our success depends on people. The people who shop with us and the people who work with us.
>
> If our customers like what we offer, they are more likely to come back and shop with us again.
>
> If the Tesco team find what we do rewarding, they are more likely to go that extra mile to help our customers.
>
> This is expressed as two key values:
>
> - No-one tries harder for customers, and
> - Treat people as we like to be treated.
>
> We regularly ask our customers and our staff what we can do to make shopping with us and working with us that little bit better.

For further information, see www.tesco.com.

The question is, why haven't all retailers got into this way of thinking? Certainly, the structure of traditional retailing, even if it uses branding to convey its values, often has brand ownership solely parked in the marketing department. Many retail marketing directors have said that their area of control is very limited. For example, developing a retailer's 'own-label' products, a critical part of a retail brand's distinctive offer, can be a difficult process leading to conflict with other departments. Given this situation, there is usually little chance of elevating customer service to a distinctive brand experience. What is needed is greater recognition of the power of the brand and brand experience – surely a clear lesson that retailers can learn from the successes of Amazon and Apple.

The definition of brand as a central organising principle needs to be accepted and acted on by retail leaders. H&M, Zara and Top Shop could not be the powerful brands they have become without the recognition that the technology that provides their operational speed is every bit as important in delivering the brand as fascias and store design. Too many are still constrained by their definition of retail as focusing on physical shops and products. Given the tangibility, complexity and expense of operating a shop it is clear to see why these become the organising idea, the preoccupation and the focus of the business.

However, neglecting the brand not only means that retailers become stuck in narrow thinking that largely ignores or diminishes the customer experience; it also means that they avoid addressing fundamental and vital questions. Perhaps the most important ones are: how are people changing, what channels and experience do they value, and how can we develop our brand to continue building strong relationships with current and potential customers? In an increasingly competitive and imaginative market, with traditional boundaries blurring, it is nowhere near enough for a business simply to focus on: how can we trade our shops harder?

Physical retailers are in an envious position. They have, potentially, a walking, talking, physical brand experience that can capture customers in a way that can be very difficult for virtual brands to achieve. This is also a time of opportunity to break purchasing patterns and inertia-based relationships with the right brand and offer. This can be achieved online (for example by Amazon) or physically (for example by Apple). The truth is this: there's never a better time to get it right – or a worse time to get it wrong.

Current thinking about branding

Why branding matters today

In an all-seeing digital world where the ghosts of corporate malpractice are never laid to rest, there is every incentive for companies to behave well. One of the ironies of the anti-globalisation movement, in its original targeting of global brands, was the failure to acknowledge that it is precisely because brand reputation is so important that a company will do everything to protect it – one of its most valuable corporate assets. If the ability to increase the value of that asset is the carrot for companies, then the stick is the knowledge of how worthless the once-proud names of companies such as Enron have now become.

The financial crisis that engulfed the world economy from 2008 raised the question of whether capitalism (and, by implication, the brands that symbolise it) should continue to have the freedom to operate that it has long enjoyed. However, this challenge to capitalism misses the real lesson: capitalism needs to be run more *sustainably*. It is essential for organisations to consider their economic, social, political and environmental impact, and central to this is their brand. Whether this is about product or service, retail or corporate, consumer or business-to-business, brands are demonstrably the most important and sustainable asset for any organisation. While the business's founders might leave, buildings fall down and products and technologies become obsolete, brands live on if they are managed well and allowed to be central to strategic development and management. To remain relevant, strong and valuable, a brand needs to be flexible, reflecting consumers' shifting preferences and values.

Achieving this brand flexibility means that all your people need to understand the nature of the brand and operate at all times in line with the brand values. For example, had the bankers and financiers of the first decade of the twenty-first century been measured by and given incentives to build long-term

> Branding matters because it connects the business with its customers. Even in hard times, a strong brand is the key to protection and growth.

sustainable brand value, rather than achieve short-term financial targets, the economic outcome may well have been different.

In fact, the financial services industry has always been one of the most challenging sectors for branding. Customers have traditionally been inert and less than engaged in the complexity of products, leading to seemingly passive relationships with brands. The structure of most banks and financial institutions is not focused on the company's brand promise to the customer, but on financial products and services. Even today in such organisations, brand management, if it exists at all, is generally viewed as a separate activity, usually in the marketing department and through advertising and communication materials. This is a particular problem as the executives responsible for other corporate activities and strategy often feel that branding is nothing to do with them. This attitude was revealed in a recent letter from a FTSE company chief executive stating that branding was not its main preoccupation at the moment. The implication is clear: in difficult market conditions, 'more important things' such as cutting costs and restructuring are the priorities.

Key concept

Brand value

A brand's value is a financial representation of a business's earnings due to the superior demand it creates for its products or services through the strength of its brand. There are three key components in understanding the value of a brand.

Financial analysis. We begin by forecasting the current and future revenue specifically attributable to the brand products. We subtract operating costs from this revenue to calculate branded operating profit. We then apply a charge to the branded profit that is based on the capital a business spends, versus the money it makes. This gives us a business's economic earnings.

Role of brand analysis. This is a measurement of how the brand influences customer demand at the point of purchase. This is applied to

continued on next page ...

---

the economic earnings to arrive at the revenue that the brand alone generates (branded earnings)

Brand strength score. This is a measure of the brand's ability to secure demand, and therefore earnings, over time. Securing customer demand typically means achieving loyalty and advocacy as well as maintaining a price premium. Our method generates a discount factor that adjusts the forecasted brand earnings for their riskiness based on the level of demand the brand is able to secure. We calculate brand strength by assessing the brand's performance against a set of critical factors.

Source: Interbrand.

Proving this point by exception is HSBC, 'the world's local bank'. This business managed to weather the financial maelstrom from 2008 by striving to embody its brand promise ('the world's local bank') and focusing on customers with cross-border banking requirements as well as those in emerging markets. The need for a strong brand has long been accepted at the highest levels of HSBC, although in its industry it doesn't have to do too much to be ahead of the competition. As many retailers know (and many banks do not), branding matters because it connects the business with its customers.

Indeed, the trust that was eroded from financial institutions in 2008 made branding more important than ever to banks as customers reconsidered their relationships. A recent study found that the role branding plays in influencing choice between brands in financial institutions is now equivalent to that of electrical appliances. Addressing the brand from a standing start will inevitably take time. Brands like HSBC that recognise the ongoing and constant commitment required to build the brand as an asset have an inevitable advantage. All organisations have a brand, but they don't all manage their brands with the vigilance and commitment that assure long-term success.

Clearly, branding is often viewed as a discretionary cost and a simple matter of expensive logo twiddling. This can be caused by the brand not being given a demanding enough agenda, allowing it to be perceived as a soft business asset. Brand valuation allows the brand to gain an economic recognition that allows it to coexist with other business assets and, as such, drive its own agenda for investments made on rigorous KPIs (key performance indicators) that embrace the demands for return on the investment. To equate branding with superficial cosmetics is the equivalent to saying that we're not interested in our customers, or we're not interested in generating sustainable wealth. This dismissive attitude means that organisations will not fully appreciate where they can cut costs while minimising the impact on customers' expectations and, therefore, on revenue. Even in hard times, a strong brand is the key to protection and growth.

The economic importance of brands

All of the economic evidence points to the importance of brands and branding. While the brand is clearly one of an organisation's intangible assets, this does not make its economic contribution and importance any less real. For example, the intangible element of the combined market capitalisation of Standard & Poor's top 500 companies has risen to around 80 per cent, from a 30 per cent share 20 years ago. The brand element of that value amounts to around one third of the total, confirming the brand as the most important single corporate asset.

Let's focus on that point for a moment. Given that the brand can be the single most valuable asset, it begs the question: Why do organisations often fail to take branding more seriously? We shall come back to this question after looking at more examples of the significance of branding.

So globally, brands are estimated to account for around one third of all wealth, and that is just looking at their commercial definition. Interestingly, some of the world's most recognised and influential brands are not-for-profit organisations, such as Oxfam and the Red Cross. Yet this is an aspect of global brands that is all too rarely considered in the public debate about brands and branding. A strong brand quickly and easily connects with customers or, in the case of not-for-profit brands, other constituents and stakeholders.

The economic importance of brands on a national and international stage is undeniable. The 100 most valuable brands in 2008 were worth over $1.2 trillion. In terms of GDP, their combined worth would make them the 11th biggest country in the world, ahead of India and just behind Brazil. If the financial clout wielded by these companies makes some commentators nervous, it should not. The owners of brands are also highly accountable. If a brand delivers what it promises, behaves in a responsible fashion and continues to innovate and add value, people will continue to vote for it with their wallets, their respect and even their affection. If, however, a brand begins to take its position for granted and becomes complacent, greedy or less scrupulous in its corporate practices, people will stop voting for it, with potentially disastrous effects for the brand and its owner. This acts as a check on the potential excesses and harm claimed by some commentators.

From an investor's perspective, the brand provides a reliable and stable indicator of the future health of a business. Looking at brand value, equity measures and audience relationships will give a more complete and realistic basis for the value of a company than short-term financial results, which often reflect short-term priorities. A study by Harvard and South Carolina universities compared the financial performance of the world's most valuable 100 brands with the average of the Morgan Stanley Capital Index and Standard & Poor's 500. They found a dramatic difference in performance in favour of firms with strong brands, which gives further quantified substance to what is qualitatively obvious: strong brands mean more return, for less risk.

The social and political importance of brands

Brands, however, are not simply economic entities. Apart from the obvious social benefits of wealth creation in improvements in standards of living, there are less recognised social effects and benefits. Many of the world's most valuable brands – from Coca-Cola to Disney and Mercedes – have been around for more than 50 years. Brands are the most stable and sustainable assets in business. They live on, long after the passing of management teams, offices, technological breakthroughs and short-term economic troughs. Clearly, to deliver this sustainable wealth they need to be managed properly. By achieving sustainable wealth, companies enjoy a more reliable income. All this in turn leads to more security and stability of employment, bringing social benefits.

Furthermore, brands have considerable political significance. Apart from the fact that political parties all over the world now employ professional branding practices, there have been many articles and studies on issues such as 'Brand America'. These have looked at the role and global dominance of American brands and at how these are being used as political symbols. Although the presence of McDonald's was initially greeted enthusias-

> A powerful political aspect of brands is their ability to cross borders, binding people and cultures together more quickly and effectively than national governments, or the bureaucratic wheels of international law, ever could.

tically in the former Soviet Union as symbolic of Russia's new-found 'liberation', McDonald's was targeted by anti-American demonstrations, despite its locally sensitive approaches to tailoring product offers and practices.

An interesting development has been the launch of competitive initiatives such as Mecca-Cola, introduced in 2002 by Tawfik Mathlouthi, a French entrepreneur. This highlights the symbolic and economic importance of brands. The strongest brands have always worked at the level of personal identity. So even if Mecca-Cola has not been a substantial financial challenge to the $67 billion brand value of Coca-Cola, it has highlighted new possibilities for using a brand to express fundamental differences of view. Whatever the motivation for launching a competitive brand, though, its long-term success will depend on its ability to satisfy a critical mass of customers with its product, service and image.

Television used to be called the second superpower. Now, the internet is the new, mobile TV screen that has all but taken this role. It used to take decades or even centuries for one culture to seep into another; now, not only can lasting and transforming images of different cultures be transferred in seconds, enduring connections can also be made. The US's dominance of the television, internet and media markets has ensured that American brands (and, indeed, Brand America) still dominate global markets. While the production and servicing facilities for brands benefit from regional flexibility, those that own the brands own the greatest wealth. One of the reasons that China has not been satisfied with being the 'factory of the world' is that it recognises that 'the person that owns the brand owns the wealth'. So China is now busy trying to build its own world-class brands.

However, any successful brand must continue to understand and anticipate changes in its audiences if it is to remain successful. It is beyond irony that the internet – essentially an American invention and 'supplied' by America – has become an instrument of challenge to US brands and its institutions.

The very notion of the internet now means that brands are able to become active participants in the conversations that surround them. While engaging in such dialogues needs careful management, it is yet another way in which brands can truly come to life and show their personality and opinions. This allows brands to grow beyond their commercial agenda into a broader arena that adds purpose to their role among their stakeholders, demonstrating that they embrace the Zeitgeist of the age.

Ownership of the brand

The brand is a reflection of the way in which a business operates. For example, Apple is seen as an innovative brand because it employs innovative people who do innovative things – such as producing popular products and selling them in distinctive stores. Because of this, marketing teams by themselves tend not to have the authority over people that brand management in a service business requires. It is really only the CEO (and possibly the COO and CFO) who have the overview and overall authority to act as Chief Brand Officer.

> Branding should occupy a pivotal role in developing business strategy and making operational decisions, as brands deliver sustainable value.

This point was highlighted by a hopeful conversation I had with a marketing director who said that his ambition was to get the brand out of the marketing department. This does not mean that marketing should relinquish its power. Instead, it acknowledges that to generate maximum power the brand should be 'opened up' to the whole organisation, ensuring that everyone feels responsible and accountable for delivering the brand. This resets the role of the marketing team to an intellectual property developer and expert champion for the organisation's brand.

Branding can be a frustrating business, but it can be so powerful when handled properly. Recently, I was talking to a CEO who had just bought out a business. One of his management team had brought in a good brand consultant who worked with the executive team to establish brand values and positioning. He was genuinely surprised at the difference this new, professional focus on branding made and then used all the business levers to ensure that the branding was properly integrated within the organisation. This is how branding is able to generate the most value.

For others in an organisation, it is easy to get the impression that marketing and media professionals care more about debating the perfect 'right' answer to the value and measurement of brands than working out how that brand connects with broader management priorities, such as financial issues. To address this and persuade the rest of the organisation to take brand management seriously, it is useful for marketing professionals to speak the business language used in other departments. It is apparent to me, for example, that using the accounting language of brand valuation helps to get boards of directors to take the brand seriously. Moreover, the methodology and application of brand valuation have improved so much that it deserves to be used routinely to influence the way in which clients and internal stakeholders make investment decisions and choose operational priorities. As technology has speeded up the business environment, a clear understanding of the brand can provide a great mechanism for holding the brand on course while allowing it to pursue the fullest opportunities of an age where everything is in 'beta'.

Nevertheless, although brand management has greatly improved, there is still room for improvement. So what can organisations do to maximise the value of branding?

Succeeding with brand positioning and managing brands

Fundamentally, organisations need to align their brand with all aspects of their operations, stretching across products and services, human resources practices and corporate behaviour, environments and communications. This matters, because when customers and other stakeholders associate an identity with an organisation, they expect it to be accurate, sincere, authentic and comprehensive. For example, if I think that Apple or Google is innovative or cool, then I think that the *whole* of the organisation is innovative or cool. Anything that any part of the business does to undermine this perception

Table 7.1 Successful brand positioning

Brand	2009 Brand Value (US$m)
1 Coca Cola (United States)	68 734
2 IBM (United States)	60 211
3 Microsoft (United States)	56 647
4 General Electric (United States)	47 777
5 Nokia (Finland)	34 864
6 McDonald's (United States)	32 275
7 Google (United States)	31 980
8 Toyota (Japan)	31 330
9 Intel (United States)	30 636
10 Disney (United States)	28 447

Source: Interbrand.

affects the *whole* brand and identity of the organisation, and anything that any part of the business does to support this view benefits the whole brand and identity.

Some of the organisations that have been most successful in positioning their brands are detailed in Table 7.1.

Why we fail to take branding seriously – and what can be done about it

The challenges of branding exist at two levels. First, we need to champion the real meaning and value of brands and branding among board members. This means expressing the importance of brands in financial, boardroom language and confronting the scepticism that exists about the 'brand thing'. Any organisation wanting to add value needs to think of itself as a brand and its leadership needs to be brought on side. A brand can be a leadership team's best ally as it provides a shorthand and clarity for their directions that sinks into the culture of the

Fundamentally, organisations need to align their brand with all aspects of their operations, stretching across products and services, human resources practices and corporate behaviour, environments and communications.

business and can be replicated for the long term. In this context, leaders need to recognise their roles as being stewards of the brand, building its equity and legacy for future generations to profit from.

However, in order to do this, we need to demonstrate vividly what it actually means to use the brand as an organising idea and explain the benefits in terms of effectiveness and efficiency. Branding needs to form the basis on which products and services are developed; it needs to inform people's behaviour, decisions and communications, both internally and externally.

Detailed in Table 7.2 are some of the main challenges or issues that organisations can address so that branding succeeds and maximises the potential of the business.

Meeting the challenges of managing a brand

There are several perennial, fundamental issues to consider when managing brands, as well as issues that are more complex or involved. For example, as well as ensuring that a brand is legally protected, it is essential to consider the role of visual and verbal brand identity in engaging audiences together with the increasingly complex area of brand communications. The growth of modern public relations has highlighted the need to ensure that internal and external messages are consistent in the way they represent the brand to the public (for further information see Chapter 9 on public relations).

When maximising the value of brands in the future, there needs to be more focus on several issues:

- *Understanding the brand's value and attributes.* A focus on brand value – specifically, measuring performance on the basis of the brand value added – can build momentum, provide focus on the right issues and create sustainable growth. It also provides crucial management information for mergers, acquisitions and divestments. Few mergers currently deliver long-term shareholder value, largely because of an over-emphasis on financial elements and practical operations. A greater focus on brand value would help mergers succeed as well as generating real organic growth.
- *Being clear about the brand's positioning.* Clarity of vision, values and overall positioning are often given insufficient attention. Many corporate and

brand visions are interchangeable, bland and viewed with cynicism. In an over-communicated world populated by corporate hyperbole, a lack of clarity will substantially reduce effectiveness and efficiency. Clarity of strategy is one of the leading criteria by which companies are judged and this especially applies to brands.

- *Using brands as central organising principles, rather than merely products and logos.* The success of experience-based brands at building strong customer relationships, in contrast to solely product-based brands, argues strongly for every brand to think about its total 'chain of experience' and customer touch points. These include every personal contact, visual identity and communications, the product, packaging, PR, the in-store environment, round-the-clock presence and availability online. Technology provides the opportunity to build an even greater sensory experience into brands through touch, smell and sound. Crucially, distinctive value will need to be added at every stage of the experience, or, at the very least, not lost.

- *Being imaginative in the way in which the brand's identity and communications are expressed.* Senior executives may not feel entirely comfortable in this area, but the ability to break through the proliferation of brands and the clutter around communications depends on imaginative, innovative and creative expression. In the developed world, audiences are knowledgeable and savvy about marketing and increasingly 'edit out' communications that they find bland, obvious, boring or irritating. Imagination needs to be applied not only to the creative message but also to the medium. For example, product placements in editorial and appropriate sponsorship of events, programmes and computer games will become ever more important. In particular, young people around the world have high expectations of brands, and are more and more difficult to reach and satisfy. They increasingly engage with brands in different ways that reflect their own values. Brands need to be seen to consciously embrace the mood of society in both the present and future tense.

- *Coordinating internal and external operations and making them transparent.* In an all-seeing digital world, and in a sharper business environment where employees at all levels can be ambassadors for or saboteurs of the company's reputation, organisations will have no choice but to be transparent in their dealings and fulfil their promises, or to have transparency

Table 7.2 Branding challenges and solutions

The branding challenge or issue ...	... And potential solutions
A lack of understanding of branding in general – and the organisation's brand in particular This is still a commonplace issue, with senior managers often not knowing what successful branding is about and simply viewing it as a cosmetic exercise. If this cosmetic approach is used to make a bad or confused business look more attractive, it is easy to see why rebranding exercises encourage cynicism. Reputation is, after all, reality with a lag effect.	**Start with a clear view of what the organisation should be about** and how it will deliver sustainable, competitive advantage, then ... **Organise all product, service and corporate operations** to deliver that view. **Use the visual and verbal elements of branding** to symbolise the distinctive view of the business. Lodge it memorably in people's minds and protect it legally with a trade mark.
A problem (including cynicism or mistrust) about the term 'brand'. This can also include misconceptions in some people's minds about the nature of brands and branding – notably a concern with its implied commercialism Misunderstanding may limit the ability of branding to be central to corporate agendas. The term 'brand' has now permeated just about every aspect of society and can be as easily applied to utilities, charities, football teams and even government initiatives as it has been in the past to packaged goods. Despite this, there seems to be a residual and stubborn belief that brands are relevant only to consumer goods and commerce. Clearly, this is nonsense: every organisation has consumers of some kind and some of the world's most valuable brands are business-to-business. Also, in the case of some arts and charitable organisations there can be a problem with commercial overtones, while for commercial organisations working in the business-to-business arena, or in heavy or technical services, there may be concerns that branding feels too soft and intangible to be relevant.	**Focus on the audiences for brands.** These can be consuming audiences, influencing audiences or internal audiences. All of these audiences need to be engaged by the brand – whether it is a product, service, corporate or not-for-profit brand – for it to fulfil its potential. Therefore, it is worth making it clear just what constitutes a brand and why it needs to be a central part of all business thinking. (This is the need for a view of the business, encapsulated by the brand, which is mentioned above.) **Remember that every successful business and organisation needs to be organised around a distinctive idea.** This is especially valuable if there are those who say: 'Yes, but why does it have to be called a brand?' To distinguish a business brand it is helpful to have some kind of shorthand (visual or verbal symbols) that can be registered and protected. To make up another term for all this would seem perverse, as branding is already in existence. **Explore why some people and organisations have an aversion to or misunderstanding of branding and then tackle the root cause.** It is a harsh truth of the arts and not-for-profit worlds that they are competing for talent, funding, supporters and audiences. Given this reality these organisations can benefit greatly by focusing their efforts and investment with the effectiveness and efficiency that brand discipline brings.

continued on next page ...

Table 7.2 Branding challenges and solutions – *Continued*

The branding challenge or issue ...	... And potential solutions
	Recognise the financial value delivered by a strong brand – in *every* sector. If the concern is that branding feels 'soft' and intangible, then remember that it is not 'soft' to use every possible competitive lever to gain every customer in a hypercompetitive international market.
Unclear ownership of the brand Whereas the more established consumer goods companies grew up around their individual brands, more complex and technical organisations are often run by people who have little experience in marketing or selling. As a result, the brand may simply be regarded as the specialist province of the marketing team, or, since the visual aspects of brands are the most obvious manifestation, brand management may be delegated to the design manager.	**Lead the brand from the top.** This challenge is not to cast aspersions on the specialist marketing and design functions, since their skills are crucial in maintaining the currency and aesthetics of the brand. However, unless the chief executive is perceived to be the brand champion, the brand will remain a departmental province rather than the driving purpose of everyone in the organisation. **Make the brand central to the organisation's success.** Although marketing is critical in shaping and presenting a brand to its audiences in the most powerful way, brands and marketing are not the same thing. For the CEO, if the brand is central to success, it makes sense for it to be the central management preoccupation. **Remember that business strategy is brand strategy – and vice versa.** Effective and efficient corporate governance is brand-driven governance. It is common for chief executives to say that people are their organisation's most important asset, but what matters is what they are organised to do. No matter how clever and talented a team is, unless the team members are united to create a distinctive and sustainable brand offer, they will be just another group of talented people, working together for a while but not creating anything of lasting value.

continued on next page ...

Table 7.2 Branding challenges and solutions – *Continued*

The branding challenge or issue ...	... And potential solutions
Lack of clarity about the tangible and intangible elements of the brand Another area of ambivalence about brands relates to their particular combination of tangible and intangible elements. The tangible area is always easier because today's senior business culture is often happier concentrating on the tangible, rational and quantifiable aspects of business. As far as quantification is concerned, brands can certainly be measured, and it is critical that they are. If a brand's financial contribution is not already self-evident, there are many formally recognised ways to put a hard and quantifiable value on it. It is the intangible, more creative, visual and verbal elements of brands that can be taken less seriously by senior management. Yet it is these elements that will engage and inspire people. When John McGrath, former CEO of Diageo, describes the creation of the Diageo corporate brand, and the vision and values to support it, he speaks warmly of the vision that clarified and inspired the company for a new future. He adds wryly that the £1 million that was paid to brand consultants for helping the company create this was a high-profile topic of media discussion at the time. This was in contrast to very little comment about the many more millions of pounds in fees and commissions that were reportedly paid to lawyers and financiers or the value of the brand to the organisation as a whole.	**Develop creativity and imagination** – these are crucial to the success of a brand. It is the easiest thing in the world for people to approach naming, product development, design and advertising ideas with an open mouth and a closed mind. Instead, brand practitioners need to have the courage of their convictions in publicly presenting new ideas, and they need to recognise that the most effective creative solution may even challenge their ownprofessional conventions.

continued on next page ...

Table 7.2 Branding challenges and solutions – *Continued*

The branding challenge or issue ...	... And potential solutions
Playing 'catch-up with the customer' Too often organisations believe that 'following the customer' is all they need do in order to succeed. There are many executives who would think this is a perfectly good strategy. However, it misses one fundamental point: playing 'catch-up with the customer' doesn't go nearly far enough in the rapidly changing markets of modern, global business.	**Understand your customers.** This should be the equivalent of breathing in business; it is an automatic function, but not something that in itself is going to make you successful. For example, in the retail sector, many brand-based thinkers have entered retailing – either physically, virtually or both – and pose a significant challenge to anyone not capable of competing through branding. The blurring of online and offline worlds (already an irrelevant distinction among most people under the age of 25) ensures that no brand is sacred in its marketplace any more. **Build strong customer relationships.** Generating the most sustainable value in the future is about having a relationship with the customer and a distinctive connection with them. Brand-based thinking forces this distinctiveness. Yet many traditional retailers still refer to 'brands' as the goods they sell in their shops, or at best the fascia over their door. They behave like a hotel for other people's brands rather than building a temple to their own.

forced on them. The internet is truly democratising and everyone's opinion is equal, be they corporate or individual. Indeed, the ability of individuals to provide agnostic opinion on brands potentially makes them a

> Any brand looking to succeed in the future will need to think and behave like a leader – not only at the basic levels of product and service distinctions, but also at the more emotional levels of creativity, values and core social contribution.

more trusted source of review. Those corporations that get it right recognise that investing in their employees translates into significantly better customer satisfaction and loyalty, two important drivers of long-term sustainable brand value.

- *Ensuring rigorous legal protection for the brand, worldwide.* The Organisation for Economic Co-operation and Development (OECD) estimates that 7–10 per cent of world trade is counterfeited. Brand owners must use the full weight of the law, quickly and publicly, to prevent value loss and degradation.

- *Creating value more sustainably.* Issues of sustainability and environmental protection are the greatest challenges of our age – and brands can help. They already generate sustainable wealth and they need to be explicit about how they deliver broader social benefits and minimise their impact on the environment. From a business perspective, this will reduce risk and minimise waste. Examples like General Electric's Ecoimagination and Marks & Spencer's Plan A have shown the benefit of presenting sustainability in an attractive, branded way, helping with consumer acceptance of sustainable lifestyles.

The future of branding

> The inability to speak with precision and certainty about the future ...
> is no excuse for silence.
>
> Alvin Toffler, *Future Shock*

It is obviously important to try to understand general trends and possibilities if we are to plan, develop and adapt brands to the future. Even the strongest brands can get stuck in a complacent time warp, overtaken by new and baggage-free competitors. From past trends, the odds might seem in favour of today's top brands still being successful in 25 years' time. In fact, over half of the 50 most valuable brands have been around for more than 50 years. However, it is difficult to see how past performance will give quite so much reassurance in the face of the extraordinary changes we are likely to see in world power and economics in the next ten years.

So, what issues and trends are likely to face brands in the future?

Staying close to consumers and market trends

The most successful technology, telecommunications and internet-based brands have already shown how quickly they can progress if they read and act on consumer and business trends in the right way. Evidence of this is provided by Microsoft, Nokia, Intel and the 'new-paradigm' global brands like

> For long-term value, brands need emotional as well as technological appeal.

Amazon, eBay and Google. Their challenge, and the challenge for the new social network brands, is to maintain their position and sustain their value. To do this, they will have to continue to innovate and, critically, to deepen and extend their brand relationships with customers well beyond the level of technological prowess. For long-term value, brands need emotional as well as technological appeal. Indeed, they will have to invest in their brand as their major sustainable competitive advantage.

An example is provided by Samsung, the South Korean conglomerate that is one of the most spectacular global brand success stories of recent years. From a brand value of just under $2.5 billion in 1997, it grew to almost $18 billion in 2008, and seems likely to continue its success. Their success accelerated when, in the mid-1990s, Samsung's managers realised the need to develop their own brand and avoid becoming just another low-price product or commodity. To build on this view of their future they viewed the digital platform as a real opportunity, invested heavily in innovating new products and, most significantly, invested heavily in their own brand. They built brand awareness worldwide and resolved to use their brand value (rather than just straight financials) as a key performance measure.

Combining global strength with local sensitivities and appeal

What is interesting is how countries outside the US (a traditional brand powerhouse) are learning the global brand game, and companies such as Coca-Cola and Nike will need to keep on reflecting their sensitivity to local cultures and habits in their management and marketing approaches. It is interesting to note that while America itself has been a strong brand for the past 50 years, standing for freedom and lifestyle aspirations, increasing familiarity and the spread of democracy have meant that these previously 'magic' qualities have lost much of their cachet and ability to inspire. American-owned brands will have to work that much harder to take a more imaginative, innovative position, as well as developing operations and communications for their brands if they are to withstand the challenge from all-comers. By contrast brands that are embedded in the cultures of the emerging economies of the East may feel that their time has now come.

Building customers' trust and developing across different sectors

The ability to transcend categories and to be trusted by consumers in whichever category it chooses to become involved will be an important property of the world's greatest brands in the future. In a hyper-competitive, over-communicated and complicated world, people will increasingly want to simplify their purchases and be more time efficient. What is more, in a world of blurring physical and virtual boundaries, any brand will have the ability to be a powerful medium and a powerful retailer – if only in virtual space. Trusted brands provide ideal navigation for consumers across sectors, and as the strongest will be able to leap into categories without having a previous product or service track record, no brand will be sacred in its marketplace any more.

For example, although it has had its financial challenges, the Virgin brand is a good example of this 'leaping' ability. It has a strong vision and values around being 'people's champion' – innovative and irreverent – and through popular support has managed to transcend markets from airlines to cosmetics, from financial services to mobile telephony and media, from soft to hard drinks and many more.

> Trusted brands provide ideal navigation for consumers across sectors.

The issue of category-defying life brands is also relevant when looking at those new or growth categories that would seem most likely to produce strong brand growth in the future. These include:

- Health and well-being
- Leisure, entertainment and 'new adventure' experiences
- Physical and emotional security
- Services for a new generation of the 'new old' (a critical trend in industrialised countries)
- Lifelong education

- Information and lifestyle issues
- Biotechnology and genetics.

Trends shaping the future of branding

Several major world trends are undoubtedly affecting brands and branding:

- *Globalisation* has certainly brought many opportunities and demonstrated the importance of branding in a highly competitive environment.
- There is also huge potential for the *development of Asian brands*, both to diversify into external markets and to compete domestically. Organisations in China and India are currently establishing their brands and this trend will, no doubt, develop strongly in the future.
- Also, given the need to attract global investment and operate in the global community, it could be argued that *nations should take advantage of brand disciplines* to project certain values to the rest of the world.
- *Corporate social responsibility* is here to stay and should have a central role in business strategy in the future.
- Also, the *digital age* and the continuing development of technology will continue to have an impact on branding.

These areas could yield entirely new global brands in the future. It may well be that the most valuable brand in the next 25 years has not been invented yet. After all, Google has progressed to a top ten global brand within ten years of its invention. However, it is equally possible that an existing, trusted brand may extend or cross into these new areas.

Engaging and communicating with customers

Service or retail brands are more likely to succeed in the future than product-based brands, which will find it harder to deepen and broaden their relationships with their audiences. This is for two reasons: first, because product-based brands (e.g. Snickers) need to invest so much of their marketing finances in retail distribution rather than spending it on consumer communication; second, because in their current form they lack the ability to control the total customer experience, and so engage their audiences as fully as they would like.

Even so, in the future expect to see more product-based brands investing in a service element. The classic example is Apple becoming a retailer, while Unilever's experiment with 'myhome', a home cleaning and laundry service, was interesting in its extension of Persil and Cif as service brands. Although it did not progress beyond its test market, it nevertheless demonstrated the company's interest in developing core brands beyond the product form. Dove Spa is another example.

Co-branding

Co-branding is another area of brand activity that is likely to increase in the future (for example, Sony Ericsson). The challenge is to be absolutely clear about the joint brand proposition, never easy in partnership.

Developing new media brands

This is also an interesting and relatively recent development, enabled by technology, where trusted sources that started as personal blogs have grown into media brands that challenge conventional media companies. An interesting example is the Huffington Post, which became popular and influential during the 2008 American elections and now has 2.5 million contributing bloggers.

Brands adapting to future social priorities

Another interesting trend is for major corporations such as Mars and Estée Lauder to launch or acquire brands that appear to be explicit 'social enterprises', allowing them to operate with no obvious brand connection with the corporate owner. For example, in 1997 Mars acquired Seeds of Change, which had been launched in 1989 with a stated purpose of preserving biodiversity and sustainable development. Estée Lauder later acquired Aveda, a brand connecting 'beauty, environment and well-being'. At a conference shortly afterwards, Leonard Lauder said that Estée Lauder was committed to phasing out synthetics entirely, following the lead of Aveda. Using new ventures of this kind as operating test-beds for new business principles indicates that major corporations recognise that business may have to be conceived and conducted differently in the future.

There is a clear need for organisations to be consistently preoccupied with maintaining the sustainable competitive advantage offered by the brand. The clarity of focus that a strong brand positioning gives an organisation will always create more effectiveness, efficiency and competitive advantage across all operations; and from a pragmatic financial perspective, research among investment communities confirms that clarity of strategy is one of the first criteria for judging companies. Crucially, organisations need to focus on the trends that are shaping the world if they are to make the most of their most valuable asset: their brand.

Key questions about branding

- How distinctive and compelling is your brand?
- How do current and potential customers view your company?
- What is your vision and strategy for your business and how, in practical terms, will your brand deliver this? What is your strategy for the brand?
- How well do employees, senior executives, the board and other stakeholders understand and support brand issues? How much of the board agenda is devoted to branding?
- Is brand value a key measurement of performance for your business? How could measurement improve? When did you last talk to the Chief Financial Officer about branding and brand management?
- Does the brand provide a focus and a guide for the way in which decisions are made and operations are structured?

continued on next page ...

- Do people understand and value the brand? Do they know what it stands for? What adjectives would be used to describe the brand? How well are these attributes communicated?
- Have you identified and prioritised those aspects of your brand that customers value most?
- How well does your brand reflect social and political attitudes, and how well does it develop and adapt?
- How will your brand change the world?

References and further information

Books

Aaker, D. (1995) *Building Strong Brands*, San Francisco, CA: Jossey-Bass.

Arnold, D. (1992) *The Handbook of Brand Management*, New York: Perseus/Random House.

Barney, J.B. (2006) *Gaining and Sustaining Competitive Advantage*, Englewood Cliffs, NJ: Prentice Hall.

D'Alessandro, D. & Owens, M. (2002) *Brand Warfare: 10 Rules for Building the Killer Brand*, New York: McGraw-Hill.

Davis, S. (2002) *Brand Asset Management: Driving Profitable Growth through Your Brands*, San Francisco, CA: Jossey-Bass.

Day, G.S. & Reibstein, D.J. (2004) *Wharton on Dynamic Competitive Strategy*, New York: John Wiley & Sons, Inc.

Kotler, P. (1999) *Kotler on Marketing: How to Create, Win, and Dominate Markets*, New York: Free Press.

Kotler, P. (2006) *Marketing Management*, 12th edn, London: FT/Prentice Hall.

Kumar, N. (2004) *Marketing as Strategy*, Boston, MA: Harvard Business School Press.

Porter, M. (2008) *On Competition*, Boston, MA: Harvard Business School Press.

Toffler, A. (1970) *Future Shock*, New York: Random House.

Trout, J. & Rivkin, S. (2008) *Differentiate or Die: Survival in our Era of Killer Competition*, Chichester: John Wiley & Sons Ltd.

Organisations and online information

American Advertising Federation, 1101 Vermont Avenue NW, Suite 500, Washington, DC, 20005-6306, USA. Email aaf@aaf.org. URL www.aaf.org.

American Marketing Association, 311 S. Wacker Drive, Suite 5800, Chicago, IL, 60606-5819, USA. Email info@ama.org. URL www.marketingpower.com.

Association of International Product Marketing & Management, 2533 North Carson Street, Suite 1996, Carson City, NV 89706, USA. Email contact@aipmm.com. URL www.aipmm.com.

International Advertising Association, World Service Center, 275 Madison Avenue, Suite 2102, New York, NY 10016, USA. Email iaa@iaaglobal.org. URL www.iaaglobal.org.

Marketing Research Association, 110 National Drive, 2nd Floor, Glastonbury, CT 06033, USA. Email email@mra-net.org. URL www.mra-net.org.

www.brandchannel.com is produced by Interbrand and provides information and an opportunity to exchange information about brands.

www.brandingasia.com provides information, tips and case examples about branding issues in Asia.

www.marketingpower.com is the website of the American Marketing Association (AMA), an international professional organisation for people involved in the practice, study and teaching of marketing. As well as setting industry standards, the AMA seeks to help marketers by providing them with information, products and services, many of which are available online, including a career centre, best practice articles, a marketer's toolkit and a newsletter. Registration is free.

Chapter 8

ADVERTISING

Jonathan Gabay
Founder, Brand Forensics

Jonathan Gabay runs Brand Forensics, advising organisations on all aspects of advertising strategy. He has worked with leading companies worldwide and has written extensively on advertising, trust, brands and leadership. For further details, visit: www.brandforensics.co.uk

Over the years advertising has changed dramatically, not only in style but in its approach, meaning and substance. What started as a tool controlled by the few to reach the many has been virtually flipped upside down, with technology enabling consumers to choose the advertising campaigns they allow into their lives. This changing relationship and shift in power require an increasingly sophisticated, subtle approach to advertising.

A journey towards excellence: How advertising has developed

The early years

During the nineteenth and early twentieth centuries, companies relied on advertising to holler out messages to encourage mass consumption. Marketers learnt that desire could be created and instilled into a market where there wasn't even a need, thanks to persuasive promotions.

Advertising certainly turned out to be a cash cow for early pioneers such as the American George P. Rowell, who published the first media directory in 1869. For a fee he placed adverts for companies and individuals with products or services to sell – including a motley and sometimes dubious range of potions, devices and strange contraptions promising to cure, grow and even encourage.

The largely unregulated advertising industry had free rein to say or claim whatever it wanted. As an example, consider Vigor's Horse-Action Saddle. It promised:

> The readiest road to health is by means of physical exercise, and the easiest and readiest mode of exercise is by using Vigor's Horse-Action Saddle – which not only provides, as Dr George Fleming, C.C., writes: 'A Perfect Substitute for the Live Horse but acts so beneficially upon the system as to be of almost priceless value. It promotes good spirits, quickens the circulation, stimulates the liver, reduces corpulence, creates appetite, cures indigestion and gout.'

Meanwhile, brands such as Pears' Soap used largely unregulated advertising to promote the British Empire's missionary zeal to educate the 'savage colonies'. One of its advertisements played on the view of the West 'civilising' native outsiders to become enlightened and fulfilled by serving the sophisticated well-to-do and gentry in America and Britain:

> The first step towards lightening the white man's burden is through teaching the virtues of cleanliness. Pears' Soap is a potent factor in brightening the dark corners of the earth as civilization advances, while amongst the cultured of all nations it holds the highest place – it is the ideal toilet soap.

The ad from 1899 featured George Dewey, an impeccably well-dressed American Navy admiral. In a smart white uniform, he was pictured washing his hands in an electrically lit cabin as his steamship sailed towards the edges of the British Empire. The advertisement's central scene is framed with views showing a fleet sailing towards new territories, as well as a picture of an unkempt black native African kneeling at the feet of a white trader. The native gratefully accepts a bar of soap from the benevolent trader.

During the First World War advertising posters ordered young men to join up, serve in the army and go into battle. In 1917, James Montgomery Flagg produced the iconic 'I Want You for the U.S. Army' Uncle Sam Poster. It was so successful that the Associated Advertising Clubs of the World adapted the theme on broadsheets to encourage citizens to buy slavery bonds and so boost the economy. Decades later, in 1971, the same poster design was used by Yale University as an anti-Vietnam war message, with the headline 'I want OUT'. Using advertising in this way reveals how much advertising became an integral part of culture, society and politics. This is hardly surprising, given that advertising works precisely because it taps into these aspects.

> In its early years, the largely unregulated advertising industry had free rein to say or claim whatever it wanted.

Inevitably, businesses could not afford to ignore such a powerful medium and it was not long before courses were offered to teach the necessary skills.

In 1923, one of the world's first PR courses was delivered by Edward Bernays at the University of New York.

The outbreak of the Second World War saw the establishment of some of the world's greatest advertising agencies, including Leo Burnett, which turned the brands of everyday consumables like corn into friendly household names. Leo Burnett helped client brands become not just one of the masses but distinctive products with mass appeal. The firm deliberately used the image of the Jolly Green Giant as a product endorsement with the instruction 'Look for the Green Giant on the label'. Today, such branding messages continue to be used by marketers in every industry, from printer suppliers to fashion brands, all urging customers to look for the image that shows the product is authentic. From its earliest days the art and science of advertising, with its emphasis on influence, persuasion and the need to alter human behaviour, were closely connected with psychology.

The psychological angle

Psychology has long played a major role in advertising's evolution. In 1957, the journalist Vance Packard published the groundbreaking book *The Hidden Persuaders*. He drew attention to the strategies and practices of big brands looking to win the minds of the public. It was Packard who first implied that advertising was full of subliminal messages. He pointed out how industry creates a yearning for new brands by introducing ever-increasing lines through planned obsolescence. However, these revelations did not, as Packard had hoped, forearm consumers against the manipulation of advertising so that they could make better choices. Instead advertising continued unabated, going from strength to strength, with consumers enjoying and embracing the process.

At the time, advertising agencies paid psychoanalysts to run the first official focus groups (then called panel reaction or group interviews). Through free-association techniques consumers were encouraged to discuss their feelings about products and services openly. Their attitudes were then neatly integrated into the product. In one case, a panel uncovered the 'insight' that housewives wanted more than merely convenience: they wanted to reclaim their skills as individuals. Consequently, products were marketed as statements of individualism. For example, cake-mix manufacturers included the unnecessary instruction to add an egg to the mixture because this made the housewife feel that she had made a personal contribution.

The recognition of this desire to understand people, uncovering personal habits, insights and preferences, marked a significant shift in advertising strategy. Products, services, commodities, even celebrities and politicians were marketed not simply by what each could actually do but how they connected emotionally with consumers, businesses and voters. In the 1970s, the Stanford Research Institute offered businesses a way to understand how to make products and services appear tailor-made for the individual, even when such items were mass produced. This strategy even led to some unusual claims, such as Fiat's television commercial in 1979 extolling the fact that its cars were 'handmade by robots'.

> From its earliest days advertising was closely connected with psychology, focusing on influence, persuasion and the need to alter human behaviour.

Academic research into advertising and marketing led to the development of ever more sophisticated techniques. Following Abraham Maslow's hierarchy of needs theory from his book *Motivation and Personality*, a consumer measurement system called Value Added Lifestyles (VALS) was devised to explain the whims and wishes of consumers. VALS segmented groups into psychological types based on the five stages in the hierarchy of needs model. Maslow claimed that despite progressing through these stages, few ever reached total achievement.

The inevitability of never being totally happy with one's lot led to the next important tenet in 1970s marketing strategies: businesses continually offering new and improved products and services to replace apparently redundant ones. The constant flow of new models and upgrades meant that consumers could never feel completely satisfied. Businesses kept on profiting from consumers, who in turn kept on coveting the next best thing, and the entire process spun around and around, with companies both chasing and leading happily unfulfilled consumers to part with their money.

Ordinary people were now directly and regularly invited to complete specific questionnaires to reveal what really motivated them. This research led to the development of increasingly sophisticated advertising strategies that appreciated the differences between consumers. The Stanford Research Institute discovered a large group who refused to be defined by society, marketing or politics. Instead, they defined themselves. These were termed the 'inner directives'. For them, personal satisfaction was more important than status or money. They were self-expressive, complex and individualistic. Another group, the 'I-am-me's', were very much of the early 1980s punk era: keen to invent their own fashions and outlooks, they decided to break from tradition. 'Experientials' would try anything, from new sports to new trends. Yet another group, the 'societally conscious', were concerned with the environment, world politics and conservation.

The trinity: The growth of television, the internet and unbridled creativity

Advertising enjoyed a significant boost with the arrival and growth of television. The world's first television commercial was aired on 1 July 1941 by the watchmaker Bulova, which paid $4 for a placement on a New York station before a baseball game. The notion of positioning a brand as 'the real thing' was perhaps first globally exemplified by Coca-Cola. In this case, the 'real thing' wasn't simply the drink alone but the feelings and experiences associated with it – for example sharing a Coca-Cola with friends, enjoying a bottle on holiday or recalling the innocent taste of childhood.

Increasingly television, especially television news, has played an even greater role in influencing and unifying consumers' attitudes about their roles in society. Having witnessed the endless stream of global news coverage from Vietnam and been threatened by the likelihood of world annihilation by trigger-happy political leaders, consumers and businesses yearned to take control back into their own hands. Businesses could fulfil this need by offering new technology that enabled people to be more efficient at work and self-sufficient at home.

This situation provided the perfect opportunity for two young computer experts to liberate not only local businesses and consumers from the constraints of the establishment but, eventually, the world. Microsoft produced its first ever advertisement in 1976. 'The Legend of Micro-Kid' appeared in the journal *Digital Design* with the headline: 'Microsoft: What's a microprocessor without it?' The ad explained how Microsoft's programming languages could be used to design software for microprocessors. The cartoon featured a small microchip character, a boxer called Micro-Kid who had speed and power but grew tired because he lacked training. The other character was a cigar-smoking trainer. The Micro-Kid had a great future but needed the trainer to succeed. This new technology instigated rapid change in how we all work and live. It also meant that the world of advertising had another powerful tool at its disposal: the proliferation of computers meant that it was now starting to have greater access to people in offices and at home.

Change and creativity were everywhere and in the UK during this period two brothers, Charles and Maurice Saatchi, were the hottest talents in town. Still feeling the after-effects of the Swinging Sixties, 'free love' had led to a higher rate of conception and the UK government asked Saatchi & Saatchi for a campaign to address the problem. The firm devised an advert promoting the contraceptive pill with a poster of a miserable young man who looked pregnant. The caption read: 'Would you be more careful if it was you that got pregnant?' This blunt style was used successfully in British Conservative politician Margaret Thatcher's 1979 election campaign with a poster of an endless queue of thousands at an unemployment office. The poster's headline read 'Labour isn't working', with the tag line 'Britain's better off with the Conservatives'. Significantly, this approach marked the beginnings of the sound-bite culture, in which laconic, incisive headlines and quotations, rather than drawn-out lengthy arguments, won the day and summed up the moment. Like Dan Weiden's 'Just do it' slogan for Nike, this abrupt technique typified the 1980s' approach to life.

By the mid-1980s, Saatchi & Saatchi's advertising agency group had become the biggest in the world. *Awareness advertising* was in the ascendancy and London was the creative capital of the world. British advertising companies blanket-bombed consumers with adverts, mailings and posters reassuring them that life could be a champagne cocktail of exuberance and

> Permission advertising arrived in force during the 1990s with the rapid growth of the World Wide Web. Among the first to embrace this new opportunity was Amazon.

success. Long-term job security was exchanged for short-term job hopping and quick house buying. This was the age of the YUPPIE – the Young Urban Professional.

This situation shifted in the early 1990s with the arrival of the World Wide Web, which led to a whole new era in advertising. Web designers developed increasingly sophisticated virtual shop windows, offering personalisation by recognising web surfers and their preferences. This was the start of *permission advertising*, designed to turn strangers into friends and friends into loyal customers. Among the first businesses to feature this facility was Amazon, which appeared on the web in 1995. The company didn't make a profit until the first quarter of 2001, when it made $5 million net of all expenses; a year earlier, it had made a loss of $545 million. The web became so ubiquitous that by 2008 the Nielsen Company estimated that there were 253 million users in China alone, and 223 million American surfers (71 per cent of the American population).

Current thinking about advertising

Uncertain times: The end of an era

The global economic collapse at the start of the twenty-first century, partly seeded by the easy access to money that had begun 30 years earlier, encouraged an atmosphere of distrust against leadership and management. Shaken by the global meltdown, many people opted to take the chance and develop their own businesses. At the same time, corporate workers retracted into departmental silos, defending their careers against threatened redundancy. People have found that throughout society, old viewpoints of self-awareness, belonging, value and community have been replaced virtually overnight with new approaches celebrating a different kind of global village. Now, villages have become tribes, and people are looking for purpose and sense in their lives. Cross-border trade and open border agreements mean that people live, work and compete in a burgeoning global community, whose population grows, on average, at a staggering 6 537 935 per month (US Census Office, October 2009).

Despite conforming and capitulating to the 'process-mapped' corporate line (if only to pay off debt and keep a roof over their heads), people have become disillusioned. During the 1960s it was famously noted that no brand manager ever got fired for recommending a 30-second TV spot. By the start of 2010, as with so many other aspects of life, commercial television had fractured into hundreds of channels. Instead of simply flicking through a magazine, people can now tune into the magazine's own radio broadcast via the web, log on to

> The internet has provided marketers with an unparalleled opportunity and one they always wanted: to be part of millions of intimate conversations heard throughout the web's global chatter.

its homepage, blog its readers, download its podcast and watch its own TV show. For the first time, the media – the messenger – with trusted and easily accessible content, has become as influential as the message. (Digital marketing is explored further in Chapter 4.)

Pervasive marketing and the start of something new

At the start of the twenty-first century's second decade, the days of mass 'push marketing' have come to a complete stop. Even micro-managed 'pull marketing', where consumers 'pull' what they want when they want it, is ending. It is now the start of *pervasive marketing*, where clarified promises are communally endorsed and shared.

Several other major trends are also shaping current thinking about advertising. These include the proliferation of collaborative, user-generated content and the growth of on-demand programming (from sources such as YouTube or Tivo). As a result, a brand manager is now lucky to get a 3-second slice of the public's attention, let alone a full-blown 30-second slot.

In addition, online advertising spending on channels such as social networking sites haw overtaken traditional offline spend. At last the consumer (the surfer) feels in control of their personal media universe and able to connect with others far and wide. However, there are consequences and new challenges: controlling a global network that can instantly spread sensitive information on sites like Twitter and through blogs has become a potential public relations nightmare.

Initially, many brands wondered how best to take advantage of the new channels featuring user-generated content. Some brands recognised that, rather than posing a threat to centralised corporate or even political messages, social networking sites offer the potential for truly democratic marketing in action, ending years of paternalism or autocracy. It was an unparalleled opportunity for marketers to achieve what they had always wanted: to be part of a conversation, part of millions of intimate conversations heard throughout the internet's global chatter.

Today's pervasive marketing is establishing a new empire: one that colonises *mind space* as well as shelf space. When practised ethically and responsibly, advertising openly satisfies everyone's requirements. Marketing directors need no longer bullishly dictate and create need simply for its own sake. Neither do their teams have to be devalued as little more than suppliers of 'pretty' marketing collateral to support the 'real' business efforts of sales directors. Today, sales and marketing can work together, listening to markets with greater intent and intensity. In doing so, they can deliver what communities sincerely want and truly deserve.

This societal change has been matched with wiser regulation, promoting higher professional standards and a deeper belief in brands. Globally, heightened awareness and consciousness among consumers have created brands that are no longer mere commodities, but conduits to mutual experiences to be valued and pooled. The result is that now consumers, particularly in the developed world, are more informed, in control and better served by advertising than ever before.

The future of advertising

The implications of these changes are highly significant for the present and the future of advertising. Today, creativity is no longer confined to the size of a broadsheet or the width of a television screen. Its canvas is as broad as can be imagined and as loud as can be shouted, while also being as sincere as a whisper between a seller and a buyer or between a politician and a voter. Increasingly, markets and consumers are being reached on *their* terms by sophisticated targeting tools.

Traditional media, including newspapers as well as conventional marketing collateral such as printed brochures, are being replaced and supplemented with interactive footage and live links that are accessible and managed anywhere on diminutive devices.

The old stalwarts, such as paper-based direct mail, have been superseded by more efficient emarketing. New marketing metrics now draw on sophisticated algorithms to probe surfers' interests, values, ethics, lifestyles and cultural attitudes towards brands. Marketing directors are business leaders who set standards by the way they act.

This brings us back to the place where this chapter started: *horsepower*. Not the horsepower promised by Vigor's Horse-Action Saddle advert in the nineteenth century, but rather the real horsepower of action, drive and energy. Across the globe, students are learning that advertising isn't merely about getting people to turn towards a message but to embrace, retain and proliferate it. Their qualifications energise them to sell, inform, inspire and encourage individuals, communities and corporations to mature and prosper.

Employers, students and advertising professionals can be confident that in the future careers won't simply be based on best practice alone. They will

> Creativity is no longer confined to the size of broadsheet or the width of a television screen. Its canvas is as broad as can be imagined and as loud as can be shouted, while also being as sincere as a whisper between a seller and a buyer or between a politician and a voter.
>
> Advertising isn't merely about getting people to turn towards a message but to embrace, retain and proliferate it.

be informed by rich experiences and lessons accumulated over many years. This understanding and insight are, of course, expanding all the time, informed by the latest ideas, techniques, realities and opportunities. The future success of advertising lies with the quality of the next generation of advertising strategists, their creativity and their ability to develop this new, equal relationship with the consumer. No company can afford to ignore this power shift towards the customer, and organisations that are able to capture and nurture this new relationship will undoubtedly prosper.

Key questions about advertising

- Do you understand your customers, what they value, believe and hope for?
- How does your offer relate to customers' needs and desires?
- Does your campaign tap into people's beliefs and aspirations?
- Do you segment current and potential customers into clearly defined groups with similar characteristics?
- How do you reach your customers – how could this improve?
- Do you have the technological capability required for different campaigns?
- How do you maintain energy and enthusiasm in your team?
- How do you promote the creative environment that is necessary for developing successful advertising campaigns?
- Do you and your colleagues keep up to date with the latest advertising skills and techniques?
- Do you set aside time to review your current advertising strategy and consider future approaches?
- Do you understand how your marketing and advertising work supports the business strategy and brand?
- How often do you communicate with other departments – both to find out their plans and priorities and to discuss your ideas with them?
- When was the last time you talked to a customer?

Further information

Books

Gabay, J. (2009) *Soul Traders: How Honest People Lost Out to Hard Sell*, London: Marshall Cavendish.

Kotler, P. (1999) Kotler on Marketing: How to Create, Win, and Dominate Markets, New York: Free Press.

Kotler, P. (2006) Marketing Management, 12th edn, London: FT/Prentice Hall.

Moore, G.A. (2002) *Crossing the Chasm: Marketing and Selling High-tech Products to Mainstream Customers*, Chichester: Capstone.

Packer, N.T. (2008) *Internet Marketing: How to Get a Website That Works for Your Business*, Tadworth: Elliot Right Way Books.

Ries, A. & Trout, J. (1994) *The 22 Immutable Laws of Marketing: Violate Them at Your Own Risk*, New York: HarperCollins.

Timm, P.R. (2001) *Seven Power Strategies for Building Customer Loyalty*, New York: Amacom.

Trout, J. & Rivkin, S. (2008) *Differentiate or Die: Survival in our Era of Killer Competition*, Chichester: John Wiley & Sons Ltd.

Zyman, S. (2000) *The End of Marketing As We Know It*, New York: HarperCollins.

Organisations and online information

Advertising Age, Crain Communications, Inc., URL www.adage.com.

Adweek, VNU Business Media, URL www.adweek.com.

American Advertising Federation, 1101 Vermont Avenue NW, Suite 500, Washington, DC, 20005-6306, USA. Email aaf@aaf.org. URL www.aaf.org.

American Marketing Association, 311 S. Wacker Drive, Suite 5800, Chicago, IL, 60606-5819, USA. Email info@ama.org. URL www.marketingpower.com. An international professional organisation for people involved in the practice, study and teaching of marketing. As well as setting industry standards, the AMA seeks to help marketers by providing them with information, products and services, many of which are available online, including a career centre, best practice articles, a marketer's toolkit and a newsletter. Registration is free.

International Advertising Association, World Service Center, 275 Madison Avenue, Suite 2102, New York, NY 10016, USA. Email iaa@iaaglobal.org. URL www.iaaglobal. org.

Marketing Research Association, 110 National Drive, 2nd Floor, Glastonbury, CT 06033, USA. Email email@mra-net.org. URL www.mra-net.org.

Chapter 9

PUBLIC RELATIONS

Paul Mylrea

Head of Press and Media Relations, British Broadcasting Corporation and 2011 President, Chartered Institute of Public Relations

Paul Mylrea is responsible for the BBC's approach to press and media relations, leading the BBC Press Office and providing strategic and editorial leadership of key reputational issues. As well as being the BBC's official spokesman he is also as a member of the Communications Steering Group, playing an active role in the leadership and development of communications across the BBC.

During a distinguished career he has worked as Director of Communications for the UK Department for International Development (DFID) as well as holding senior positions at Oxfam, Transport for London and Reuters. He is a Visiting Fellow at Bournemouth University's Media School.

Although sometimes misunderstood, engaging with 'publics' and building positive relationships have always been challenging and vital activities for organisations and individuals. The reasons for public relations remaining critical persist and, in the twenty-first century, are driven by globalisation, technological change and the need for an ethical approach in life and work.

How public relations has developed

Public relations (PR) is an essential aspect of organisational life because it is about creating dialogue and generating understanding between an organisation and its publics. It facilitates a relationship and enables people to participate in a genuine conversation, with all that implies. It is the discipline that looks after reputation. Just as an individual might engage in a conversation or dialogue to express a view, persuade, influence, enquire, challenge, manage expectations or understand, all the while staying true to the individual's own values, so it is with PR at an organisational level.

Given this definition, it is easy to see why PR has grown steadily in relevance and impact throughout the last century. The means, motive and opportunity for organisations to engage in dialogue about an increasing range of topics have all risen steadily. For example, the phenomenal growth of the internet and social media has only added to the opportunities and potential benefits of PR. It can be argued that public relations is today more significant, impactful, necessary and beneficial than at any other time.

Given this situation, it is perhaps ironic that despite its essentially social character based on communication, engagement and influence, PR is frequently misunderstood. Sometimes derided as 'spin' or 'propaganda', a propensity to misinterpret PR has dogged the subject for decades and owes something to its origins. The discipline has existed in various forms for centuries, but in the

> Public relations is about creating dialogue and generating understanding between an organisation and its publics. It facilitates a relationship and it is the discipline that looks after reputation.

context of business and modern organisations its origins can be traced back to the early twentieth century. (An expert analysis of the origins of PR is provided by Tom Watson, Professor of PR at Bournemouth University, in Watson, 2010.)

The birth of modern public relations

Edward Bernays, who was born in Vienna in 1891 and died in the USA in 1995, is regarded as one of the earliest influences on modern public relations (see Tye, 2002). Interestingly, he was a nephew of Sigmund Freud, the 'father of psychoanalysis', and at least part of the reason this label has lasted for Freud was because of the influence and activity of his nephew. Opinion is divided about Bernays' legacy: some regard him as a PR genius, while to many others he was little more than a propagandist.

What is clearer, however, is the range of forces and theories that have formed modern public relations. These include issues such as education and corporate social responsibility, as well as the impact of technology, globalisation, business ethics and issues management. The following are significant milestones in the development of PR:

- Nineteenth century: this period was widely regarded as the era when press agents, publicists and showmen like Phineas T. Barnum enthralled the public. They showed what could be accomplished with publicity based on technology and creativity.
- 1900–30: during this era PR became established. No longer viewed as mere 'showmanship', it came to be seen as a valuable and indispensable tool for communicating and engaging with people. The development of PR during this time was led by bold pioneers including Edward Bernays, Ivy Lee (adviser to John D. Rockefeller) and Arthur Page.
- 1930–50: PR became more sophisticated, largely driven by developments in technology – notably the worldwide growth of radio and television broadcasting – and politics. Immediately before and during the Second World War government communications (and propaganda) became widely established. This took PR's existing techniques and furthered them, for example by using opinion research. At this time an activity that is about researching

opinions, communicating and engaging people came to the attention of government. It was in 1948 that Britain's then Institute of Public Relations, now the Chartered Institute of PR, and America's Public Relations Society of America were founded as professional bodies for practitioners.

- 1950–70: PR focused on media relations and events and many countries established professional bodies for the advancement of PR. In the 1960s major PR consultancies became established, beginning in the USA, and the profession attracted journalists in significant numbers for the first time.
- 1970–90: now firmly established worldwide, three trends emerged that shape the practice of PR. First, academic study of the subject, notably in the USA and Germany; second, the continued growth of corporate PR work; and third, an emphasis on rigour and results with work beginning on measurement and evaluation. By the 1980s the industry began to grow rapidly, with consumer PR being widely used by major brands. In the UK, the Conservative government's privatisation programme also successfully used PR. It was also in 1984 that James Grunig, now at the University of Maryland, codified his four-model theory of PR. The four models describe different approaches to public relations. Press agentry, as with Barnum, is working to get your client in the newspapers. It is still the staple of celebrity publicists today. Public information is more about the distribution of information of use to people. Again, it is still a standard tool, particularly for some public bodies, but it depends less on understanding audiences and more on putting out information. The 2-way asymmetrical model is where practitioners use research and analysis to understand their audiences and what motivates them. This is familiar territory to marketers and advertisers. However, it is more about persuasion than two-way communication. The 2-way symmetrical model sits at the top of the hierarchy, pointing to the use of communication to negotiate with publics, resolve conflict, and promote mutual understanding between an organisation and its publics. At its heart is a view that everyone should benefit from the communication, not just the initiating or contracting party. It may sound idealistic, but this is the foundation of good PR and is inherently suited to a social media age.
- 1990–2010: the three forces of technology, globalisation and ethics began to drive the growth of PR and shape its character. During this period strong global economic growth was punctuated by sharp recessions. At least partly

as a result of these developments, PR firms and corporate communications departments became increasingly efficient, coordinated and global. Not-for-profit PR also became established, highlighting the connection between ethics and public relations. During the 1990s PR 1.0 began with the internet becoming popular worldwide and the new technologies of the decade supporting the global growth, efficiency and effectiveness of PR. In the 2000s this became PR 2.0, with greater interaction and engagement achieved, notably through social media.

The global growth of public relations

The occasional portrayal of PR in the media as a glamorous profession – based more on sitcoms such as *Ab Fab* than the reality of the business – has undeniably attracted many people, particularly over the last two decades. But behind this public image the profession has been developing a growing body of knowledge about the practice of public relations. This encompasses a range of views including psychological, sociological, philosophical and economic perspectives. The result has been to deepen the knowledge, expertise and credibility of the subject. There are now over 70 degrees or parts of degrees, including PhDs, concerned with the practice of professional PR. In recent years the body of knowledge about the subject has been helped considerably by the work of dedicated experts and researchers, largely from Europe. This includes expert researchers and authors such as Jacquie L'Etang, Inger Jensen, Dejan Vercic, Betteke van Ruler, Ralph Tench and Liz Yeomans.

Towards the end of the twentieth century several developments reinvigorated the work of public relations. First, high-profile gaffes, misjudgements and sheer unprofessionalism resulted in a widespread backlash against PR. One example was the widely reported remark by a UK political officer in the aftermath of the terrorist disaster of 9/11 that it was 'a good day to bury bad news'. In the USA, executives at the Texas energy firm Enron lied and gave false information on a grand scale. This not only damaged the company, it virtually destroyed it. The most significant PR lesson from both of these examples is simple: what is right in business terms is also the right thing to do for public relations. PR cannot be 'grafted on' to an organisation or approach that is unethical or lacking integrity. While PR works with organisations, groups and individuals to understand and manage the impact of their actions, it only succeeds and endures when it is ethical. When it comes to understanding public relations, this simple fact is often overlooked.

Another reason for PR taking centre stage was that it failed to manage its own profile and, at times, became the story alongside the issue it was promoting. For example, the overwhelming electoral success of New Labour in the UK's

> 'Reputation has a direct and major impact on the corporate well-being of every organization, be it a multinational, a charity, a government department or a small business.
>
> That is why the professionalism of those people who guard and mould reputation – public relations practitioners – is so important.'
> Chartered Institute of Public Relations

1997 general election was in part attributed to the party's media management skills. (In the UK, this approach first became noticeable with the Conservative Party's 1979 election campaign, which also made widespread use of the media.) However, there was an increasing sense of unease in parts of British society about 'spin' and the feeling that emotions and political views were being manipulated. Similar concerns have arisen in other Western democracies, notably the USA, where massive, multifaceted media campaigns have become the norm, overshadowing and sometimes eclipsing thoughtful, rational debate about policy and performance.

A third reason for the renewed profile of public relations has been the development of the internet and new media, particularly since the 1990s. Shell was one of the first companies to take a hit in the new media war. The company was taken by surprise in 1995 when environmental activists at campaigning organisation Greenpeace successfully protested against the sinking of the redundant Brent Spar oil platform. Largely as a result of this event, Shell International developed an online strategy that included monitoring what was being said about the company in cyberspace.

All of these issues highlight several simple, vital truths about public relations that are frequently overlooked, especially by people outside the discipline. PR is not solely concerned with promoting a product. It is about influencing the conversation that a leader, advocate or organisation has with others. The influence is two way – both influencing publics but also responding to their views, as Grunig suggests in his final model. This fact has an important implication and consequence: PR does not have *control* over its messages.

In many ways, an industry that is about public perception has deserved a much better public profile. In recent years, the reputation of PR and its ability to deliver have started to change significantly for several reasons, notably the rise of globalisation, technology and ethics.

The state of the art: Successful public relations

Interestingly, of the people that have typically brought PR into disrepute, surprisingly few have actually been PR professionals. Most have been politicians, advertisers, journalists, civil servants, business executives and others. One conclusion may be that PR is perceived as being 'easy' or simple – specifically, that it is easy to control a message. In reality, it is almost impossible to control a message. This was the case even in the early days of Edward Bernays' activities and it is certainly true now, at a time when organisations, societies and individuals are profoundly influenced by technology and globalisation, and when they value an ethical approach as much as ever. This leads to several questions:

> PR is not solely concerned with promoting a product. It is also about influencing the conversation that a leader, advocate or organisation has with others. This fact has an important implication and consequence: unlike sales and marketing, PR does not have control over its messages. It is about influencing and this requires a dialogue.

- What are the principles of great PR?
- What is the impact on public relations of technology, globalisation and ethics in the present and the future?

The principles of great PR

First, PR is about dialogue, not control. Unlike other related activities in the area of sales and marketing, PR does not control its messages. It is about *influencing* and this requires a dialogue with its publics. This dialogue occurs through multiple channels and the result is a perception that builds into a single brand. Dialogue also results from knowledge of the external environment and the ability to be heard internally, within the organisation. This lack of complete control is why, for example, non-governmental organisations have long understood the need for influence, dialogue and reputation management.

Key concept

Professional PR

The principles of great PR are reflected in the award of Chartered Practitioner by the CIPR (the Chartered Institute of Public Relations). This was first awarded in 2009 to CIPR members with the required level of experience, knowledge and insight. The rigour involved in awarding chartered status both to the CIPR and, through the Institute, to suitably qualified professionals, highlights both the maturity and the significance of the profession.

Closely related is the fact that great PR engages with people instead of avoiding or ignoring them or their issues. The key to success is to engage, even when things aren't right and *especially* if there are problems or concerns. PR is about relationships with people who agree and disagree and this requires relationship building, a positive, two-way discussion, and a willingness to take key messages to the top team.

This leads to another important principle: PR needs to be strategic and actively supported at senior levels in an organisation. Clearly, the messages that an organisation gives have to be genuine and consistent; for this reason, they need the support of executives at the very top of the business. Senior executives need not only to understand and believe what is being said, but also ensure consistency and appropriate action throughout the organisation. Two other issues spring from the strategic nature of PR: it requires internal support as well as an external focus; and it involves continuous change, improvement and an ability to make tough choices. It is important to remember that PR has an internal dimension as well as an external one. Communication, dialogue and understanding are as important within an organisation as they are outside – sometimes, even more so.

> PR works by enabling organisations to manage and understand the impact of their actions on their publics. It matters because a reputation that has taken years to build can be lost overnight.

PR requires change and tough choices. Changing and improving what you do or your organisation does is an essential aspect of PR. After all, PR is about building relationships and from time to time these require action as well as listening. Interesting examples are provided by the adoption of the Sarbanes-Oxley corporate governance legislation in the USA, and by the public interest in the UK in 2009 in the expense claims of members of parliament. In both instances, listening and understanding public concerns were simply not enough: behaviour had to change and improvements needed to be made.

These examples highlight another important truth about PR: disclosure is important. The example of MPs' expenses and the concerns about corporate activities that gave rise to the Sarbanes-Oxley legislation show that you cannot manage relationships with the public selectively and that disclosure matters. Not only is disclosure usually the ethical thing to do, it is also sensible, given that technology and globalisation will converge to ensure that a message given at one specific time and place to one group will spread to other groups at other times.

PR can include moments to tell as well as to listen, particularly at times of pressure or crisis. For example, after the terrorist bombings on the transport system in London on 7 July 2005, Transport for London (TfL) worked to provide information, clarity, openness and reassurance. Terrorism thrives on fear and uncertainty and in these circumstances public relations has a valuable role to play by explaining the realities of the situation, providing information and dispelling fear. PR also succeeded at this time by putting a face on the issue and showing people that TfL was on the side of the travelling public.

Evaluation and the measurement of PR communications are also vital principles. The challenge is to be able to attribute changes in attitudes and behaviour to specific PR activities. The nature of PR requires it to be rigorous, proactive and insightful, qualities that benefit from effective measurement. Closely linked is the need to be able to demonstrate the long-term benefits of engagement. This is much harder to measure and is, perhaps, an area for further development in the future, possibly with new technology.

Technology: Creating and improving relationships

Technology is continuing to shape public relations in profound and far-reaching ways, providing both opportunities and threats. In particular, technology is transforming the way in which people access, find and use information. We can now gain access to an unrivalled range of images, information, knowledge, people, products and views through Twitter, YouTube, blogs, podcasts, the internet, apps and a myriad of other technology-based services. In these circumstances the traditional role of public relations professionals as media gatekeepers is changing profoundly.

Above all, technology is affecting the way that organizations engage in dialogue, build relationships and connect with their publics. Audiences have become much more capable and savvy with all types of digital media and PR has to evolve with them. Gauging and influencing public opinion requires an ability to use online media – and this can include individual blogs. There are now many more potential influencers who need to be recognized and considered and one of the priorities for PR professionals is to harness the potential offered by social media.

In fact, social media is a valuable, vital tool because it facilitates dialogue and brings the openness that is at the heart of successful PR. Openness and transparency not only result in good public relations, they matter because they enable

> The perfect storm occurs when globalisation combines with technology. This enables people to communicate across time zones, with respect for authority weakening with distance and time. In this situation, integrity, dialogue and trust matter more than ever.

people to build trust, reputation and support. The difficulty with this is the difficulty with any relationship: it requires a genuine commitment and positive regard for the other person or people. In short, it needs effort. Social media requires us to establish trust, rapport and dialogue. This is achieved by what you say, what you do and what others are inclined to say about you.

An interesting example is provided by the classic case of Shell, Greenpeace and the disposal of the Brent Spar oil platform mentioned earlier. Initially, people trusted Greenpeace, characterised as the small, ethical organisation concerned with environmental issues on behalf of everyone, versus Shell, caricatured as the longstanding, multinational corporation whose sole concern was the ruthless pursuit of profit. Unfortunately, Greenpeace's science was largely flawed: of all the possible ways of disposing of the platform Shell's approach was one of the least damaging to the environment. Although Shell initially suffered and, in common with many other oil companies, has not always had a blameless record, some journalists came to feel that they had been duped by Greenpeace.

As well as facilitating relationships, technology is also benefiting public relations by changing the way people work. PR professionals are now able to do more, working more productively and effectively than ever before. Technology is changing the context as well as the tools available for public relations. Highlighting this point is the wide range of online media services. These include web-enabled video news releases, public opinion surveys, blogs, media monitoring and Really Simple Syndication (RSS). There are now more opportunities and ways to build relationships and engage in dialogue, and more ways for your reputation to be harmed, more quickly, if you do not.

Improving PR relationships: Blogging

A good example of the nature of great PR and the ability for technology to enable people to build relationships is shown by the twenty-first-century phenomenon of *blogging*. There are

Blogging and liaising with bloggers is about building relationships and this means that it is highly personal. Blogging relies on an ability to participate in intelligent conversations, not only with journalists but with everyone who helps define your brand.

several simple rules for people who want to communicate a brand story through a PR blog. (For further information see Wreden, 2007.)

First, blogs are personal: they make clear the blogger's passions and viewpoint rather than simply pitching an idea. This understanding then extends to the way in which a PR professional approaches a blogger, with the need for short, concise emails, an informative subject line and an absence of attachments. 'Hyping' or pitching is counter-productive: if you wouldn't say it in the context of a new professional relationship, then don't say it to a blogger. If you are trying to develop a relationship with a blogger it is also worth remembering that most bloggers are interested in the power of an idea or a point of view, rather than their audience. Above all, engage in an intelligent, informed dialogue; focus on quality, not quantity; and make the email feel as if it is from a knowledgeable best friend, not a direct mail house.

Technology has implications for the way in which messages are developed and delivered. This links closely with the previous point and delivering messages is clearly an important part of the work of a PR professional. A significant example is the rise of 'mash-up' media where two or more sets of data are combined. Also, research can now be more global, in depth and faster than ever before.

Technology is reshaping organisations' structures, cultures and management, changing the way in which PR is managed internally. One of the most interesting effects has been that digital communication is flattening organisational hierarchies (emails and weblinks are no respecters of status). People with greater access to more relevant data than ever before are likely to be less frustrated, more engaged and more productive. They no longer require command-and-control management structures (if they ever did).

Digital communications also make it easier to share information externally as well as internally, with the result that organisations can be more open and transparent, ensuring greater understanding between diverse groups as well as overcoming the challenges of time and distance. Technology is enabling greater collaboration and increasing decentralisation. In short, as online technologies become more popular, they are resulting in even greater openness and transparency.

It is worth remembering that the perfect storm occurs when globalisation combines with technology. This enables people to communicate across time zones, with respect for authority weakening with distance and time. In this situation, integrity, dialogue and trust matter more than ever. In fact, the more complex the world becomes, the more important it is to engage in dialogue with everyone: those who agree, those who disagree, and those who are undecided. (For further information about the nature of social media see Chapter 4 on digital marketing.)

Globalisation and PR

Globalisation remains a remarkable force for change, largely driven by technology and trade. Now, more than ever before, publics and audiences are global and need to be managed globally. A practical example of this is again provided by Transport for London which, following the terrorist bombings in London on 7 July 2005, provided press briefings in three languages and online, recognising that its publics were international. Many types of organisation now interact with publics outside their country of origin. This fact combined with the rise of globalisation means that several issues are increasingly significant for successful PR:

> Openness and transparency matter not simply because they result in good public relations; they matter because they enable people to build trust, reputation and support.

- Globalisation is increasing the scope and complexity of relationships. Trade, environmental issues, politics, security, information flows, cultural exchanges and social networking are just a few of the forces that are increasing the complexity of relationships.
- There is much greater interdependence and connectivity among individuals, organisations and societies. The complexity of relationships is further compounded by the ease with which people can make common cause across traditional boundaries and barriers.
- Cross-border issues have implications for the coordination and control of public relations. The challenges that result include how to be both global and local; whether to integrate PR in one coordinated department or to decentralise; and how to manage the work of different agencies across borders. The solution is to find the right balance between being global and

local, centralised and decentralised, as well as ensuring that all messages are consistent while allowing for differences in emphasis.

- The spread of globalisation means that information, issues and reputations now cross borders easily. The literature of public relations contains prominent examples of firms whose reputations and profits in one market suffered because of actions in another. For example, from BP's share price to Firestone tyres, Toyota cars, Mattel toys and Perrier mineral water, organisations are finding that events in one market have great potential to affect their business elsewhere.

- Cross-cultural awareness and diversity are vital. There are interesting examples of diverse approaches to public relations. For instance, in Japan there is an element of *kou-chou* (or public hearing), with PR professionals making an effort to know what their publics think before changing management strategies. Similarly, Japanese, Indian and South Korean professionals typically use PR to disseminate positive information that will enhance the image and reputation of their organisation.

- Clearly, if audiences are now global then the way in which messages are delivered – and even the context of the message itself – needs to be tailored so that dialogue can continue and relationships can develop. This issue is especially challenging for any multinational organisation. The keys to success are to build relationships with diverse publics both locally and globally, and to appreciate the social, political, economic and cultural contexts relevant to those publics.

Building relationships with a diverse array of people requires specific knowledge, skills and personal attributes (this information is explored in detail by the Tilford Group on Diversity and Multiculturalism at Pittsburg State University; see http://faculty.pittstate.edu/~ananda/Tilford.html). The knowledge needed by PR professionals includes:

- Cultural self-awareness and the ability to recognise one's own cultural values and identity
- An understanding of different cultures and diverse ethnic groups
- Recognition of the ways in which diverse groups around the world are affected by social, political, economic and historical events.

Key concept

Professionalism

The Chartered Institute of Public Relations (CIPR) is a UK-based organisation that has established a code of conduct for anyone involved in PR. As well as highlighting the need for integrity, competence, confidentiality, transparency and avoiding conflicts of interest, the code begins with several clear principles:

1 Maintain the highest standards of professional endeavour, integrity, confidentiality, financial propriety and personal conduct.
2 Deal honestly and fairly in business with employers, employees, clients, fellow professionals, other professions and the public.
3 Respect the customs, practices and codes of clients, employers, colleagues, fellow professionals and other professions in all countries where they practise.
4 Take all reasonable care to ensure employment best practice, including giving no cause for complaint of unfair discrimination on any grounds.
5 Work within the legal and regulatory frameworks affecting the practice of public relations in all countries where they practise.
6 Encourage professional training and development among members of the profession.
7 Respect and abide by this Code and related Notes of Guidance issued by the Institute of Public Relations and encourage others to do the same.

See www.CIPR.co.uk for further information.

- An understanding of the ways in which changing demographics affects cultures and the implications of demographic change
- An understanding of political, economic, social and technological factors that do and could have an impact on organisations
- Assimilation of external factors and development of strategy accordingly

The skills needed by PR professionals include:

- Cross-cultural communication, including non-verbal skills
- Team working and the ability to engage and mobilise people from different diverse groups to achieve a common goal
- The ability to resolve cultural conflicts and use critical thinking skills
- Research and evaluation skills.

The personal attributes needed to build relationships with a diverse group of people include:

- The flexibility and capacity to adapt to a fast-changing world
- Empathy, respect and an appreciation of differences in others.

Just as the challenges can be global, so too are the solutions: do the right thing, be open and constructive, and engage with people positively. In a world that is increasingly globalised and networked, one traditional aspect of public relations remains as important as ever: the need for ethics.

The need for ethics at work

The role of PR in influencing and persuading means that an ethical approach is essential. No one will be influenced for long or in a way that is sustainable by someone that lacks integrity. After all, who wants to be conned? Where it is successful, PR maintains external reputation and provides guidance, insight and judgement on actions, behaviours and choices.

These are not abstract considerations. There are many situations in which PR practitioners will not engage for ethical reasons, but there are times when it is necessary to engage to achieve change. This is where the impact of genuine two-way communication is key. There may be issues with the way an individual, organisation or country has operated. But in order to achieve change, professional practitioners can sometimes offer stark advice that others 'inside' cannot. If this achieves lasting change, and it can be delivered in a way that is transparent and ethical, then it may be acceptable. Nevertheless, these are difficult areas that require practitioners to be aware of the pitfalls and to follow the guidelines and codes of the professional bodies.

Several universal personal attributes are fundamental to ethical public relations (discussed in detail by the Chartered Institute of Public Relations in its Code of Conduct at www.CIPR.com). These attributes include integrity, competence, confidentiality, transparency and an ability to avoid conflicts of interest. They are so significant that it is worth considering each attribute in detail:

- *Integrity* – being honest, avoiding unprofessional behaviour and possessing a responsible regard for the public interest. In practice, this means checking the reliability and accuracy of information before dissemination, and never knowingly misleading people.
- *Competence* – being aware of personal limitations, working to develop and improve one's personal skills, and being willing to collaborate or delegate.
- *Confidentiality* – respecting confidences, avoiding the use of confidential or inside information to secure an advantage or to disadvantage someone else, and never disclosing confidential information without specific permission, to protect the public interest, or if required by law.
- *Transparency and avoiding conflicts of interest* – this means conforming to accepted business practice and ethics, for example by disclosing any financial interest in a supplier.

The last century has seen the dramatic rise of public relations, shaped by globalisation, technological change and ethics. Clearly, these forces are as significant for the future of PR as they have been in its past.

Key questions about public relations

- How well does your organisation engage with and listen to its publics?
- Do your senior executives understand the nature of great PR and recognise the need for dialogue with your publics?

continued on next page ...

- Do your PR professionals have access and support at the highest levels?
- Is there the right balance between central control and decentralised action? Is the right structure in place for your PR activities?
- Who are your publics and how can you improve your dialogue and relationships with them?
- Do your communications strike the right balance between telling and listening?
- Do your public relations activities recognise the challenges and opportunities of globalisation and technology?
- Above all, is your organisation open and sincere in its communications? Does it adopt an ethical approach?

References and further information

Tye, L. (2002) *The Father of Spin: Edward L. Bernays and The Birth of PR*, London: Picador.

Watson, T. (2010) Tom Watson, professor of PR at Bournemouth University, asks what the history of PR can teach us, and provides a timeline showing key moments in PR, *PR Review*, www.prmoment.com/306/the-history-of-pr-tom-watson-from-bournemouth-university-provides-a-pr-timeline-showing-key-moments-in-public-relations.aspx.

Wreden, N. (2007) *ProfitBrand: How to Increase the Profitability, Accountability and Sustainability of Brands*, London: Kogan Page.

Chapter 10

Keith Glanfield
Foundation for Management Education Fellow, Marketing Group, Aston Business School

Keith Glanfield is Foundation for Management Education Fellow with the Marketing Group at Aston Business School. During his career he has worked in the private and the public sectors in senior commercial and marketing management positions, successfully delivering business growth in consumer, SME, corporate, public sector and international markets. Keith's research interests concern the effective strategic use and application of branding across all sectors, and in particular, the effective application of branding inside organisations.

Internal marketing is a powerful tool, with the potential to deliver high service quality and customer satisfaction. Yet in practice it is often misunderstood and overlooked, seen as little more than a perfunctory add-on. This is a missed opportunity, as marketing has so much more to offer internally, by significantly contributing to the delivery of internal marketing's substantial commercial benefits. To unlock this potential, we need to address some key issues and ask some fundamental questions. How widely understood is internal marketing, and are marketers aware of its significance and potential? How can marketing refocus and reinvent itself to achieve more for the whole company by looking internally? In particular, how can we build a single corporate brand community of consumers and service employees to deliver future commercial success?

The development of internal marketing

Over the past 30 years, substantial change has taken place in the way in which the marketing profession approaches its discipline. No longer is it enough to put the marketing plan to bed once a year, secure a budget, brief the agency and get on with delivery. In today's world, there is a need for perpetual market planning to deal with the rapidly changing needs of the consumer. The fragmentation of media has brought about continual pressure to track what activity is most effective and where the best return is coming from. And, with the advent of social media, marketers have to continually tussle to get heard and put across brand messages against all the background noise and interference that surround customers.

These are all changes that most in the profession would recognise. But, you may ask, what impact does this have on internal marketing? The answer is that these developments require us to revisit the traditional approach of simply inserting internal marketing at the end of the yearly marketing-planning cycle: it is now time to realise the full potential of internal marketing. In the past, in practice, internal marketing was a rather perfunctory affair, involving briefing the appropriate internal staff about the details (and reasons) behind the marketing activity for the coming year. In practical terms, this approach seems increasingly inadequate, begging the question: over the past three decades, has internal marketing kept pace with the substantial changes made by the profession to attune itself to the changing external environment? In particular, is it time for the marketing function to reconsider its internal role, to reinvent itself, in order to unlock future commercial success?

In answering these questions, this chapter charts the significant stages of internal marketing's theoretical development over the past 30 years. It considers the extent to which the marketing function potentially influences, and should be concerned with, the traditional theoretical form of internal marketing. It contends that, in the future, the marketing function needs to think differently about its internal role and how it supports the objectives of internal marketing: refocusing and reinventing itself to bring about improved commercial results.

Internal marketing – the popular perception

At first glance, because the phrase 'internal marketing' contains the word 'marketing', it is easily assumed that in its entirety internal marketing must, and should, be the sole domain of the marketing function. In practice, the term 'internal marketing' tends to be used as a convenient shorthand label for aspects of marketing activity that are not customer or market facing. In other words, internal marketing is viewed as those activities undertaken by the marketing function inside the organisation. That, in the main, involves the marketing function forming relationships with key internal stakeholders. The priority is to gain greater internal influence as well as commitment to marketing initiatives, such as product development and campaigns, from interested groups of employees. However, it is difficult to be more specific than this about how precisely mar-

> At its inception, internal marketing contained two central principles:
>
> 1 It is important to satisfy employees' needs before the company can satisfy the needs of its customers.
> 2 The rules applying to a company's external markets are also relevant to its internal market.

keting professionals define and deploy internal marketing in practice, as this tends to vary between organisations.

So, is this broad popular perception of the meaning of internal marketing, and its associated activities, what was meant theoretically at its inception? Does this view fit with the role that has developed through three decades of research and theoretical development? An extensive array of theory and research is present in academic literature; however, in broad terms, internal marketing has evolved through three linked but distinct stages of development (Table 10.1):

1　The internal market – employee satisfaction leads to customer satisfaction
2　Part-time marketers – service-minded and customer-orientated employees
3　Internal market orientation – internal fit with the marketing strategy.

The internal market – employee satisfaction leads to customer satisfaction

At its inception in the late 1970s, internal marketing was founded on the need for service organisations to consistently deliver high levels of service quality to customers, by better understanding the needs of employees who delivered the service. The assumption was that satisfying the needs of service employees increases job satisfaction, which in turn improves service quality. Therefore, conceptually, internal marketing is concerned with making available internal products (jobs) that satisfy the needs of a market (employees), while also satisfying the objectives of the organisation.

In operational terms, internal marketing contains two central principles. First, it is important to satisfy employees' needs before the company can satisfy the needs of its customers (Berry, 1981). Second, the rules that apply to a company's external markets are also relevant to its internal market. In its application, internal marketing is an approach to service management concerned with HR and operational practice, and concerned with recruiting, training, motivating and retaining suitable service employees. The role of the marketing function at this stage of development is limited.

Table 10.1 **Three broad stages in the theoretical development of internal marketing**

Development stage	Principles	Internal marketing activity	Marketing function's role
Internal market	Internal market of employees Job satisfaction leads to higher service quality and customer satisfaction	Service management and HR recruiting, retaining and motivating service employees, e.g. job descriptions, rewards and benefits etc.	Limited
Service employees as part-time marketers	Internal customers Service-minded and customer-orientated service employees Using 'marketing-like' thinking and activity to address the internal market, i.e. market research	Management support Training Human resource management Internal mass communication Systems and technology support Market research External mass communication	Internal briefing of external marketing and market research. Advice on development of 'marketing-like' internal activity
Internal market orientation	Develop an internal orientation to the internal market Internal orientation fitting with organisation's external market orientation to deliver objectives of marketing strategy	Internal market intelligence gathering Internal communication Response to intelligence	Influence scope and direction of internal marketing through organisation's marketing strategy. Operational delivery, affecting service quality etc., remains a matter for HR and service operations

Part-time marketers – service-minded and customer-orientated employees

The next evolution introduced the concept of the 'internal customer'. Here, the scope of internal marketing widened within the organisation to include all back-office staff, by establishing the need for internal supplier/customer relationships (Gummesson, 1999). At each step in the chain of delivering a service to an external consumer, each internal supplier transfers value to its internal customer. It is not difficult to appreciate that by satisfying these internal needs and managing the relationships well, this value will continue along the chain so that the organisation is better prepared to satisfy the needs of the external consumer. To achieve this, the objectives of internal marketing developed not only to satisfy external customers through satisfying service employees, but also to motivate the whole workforce towards service-mindedness and customer-orientated performance. Here, the internal market of employees is best motivated to adopt service-mindedness and customer-orientated behaviours by an active, marketing-like approach, where marketing-like activities are used internally.

The mix of internal marketing activities that could be deployed is based on the assumption that the organisation is relationships-based and has a network of groups. Internal marketing activity uses a mix of tools, including training, management support, empowering and enabling employees, internal mass communication, human resource management, systems and technology support and, crucially, market research and mass external communications. In managing and deploying this range of activity, the aim is to influence the attitude of employees and develop two-way communication between management and employees, with the result that employees become part-time internal and external marketers (Gronroos, 2000).

At this point there is a recognition that the marketing function's stake in internal marketing is enhanced, as employees need to understand external communications and share internal and external market research. However, the main emphasis is on the organisation adopting 'marketing-like' practices to address this internal market of employees. In this situation, much of the responsibility for developing and implementing internal marketing falls to the HR, operational and service management functions.

Internal market orientation – internal fit with the marketing strategy

Still working on the foundations of addressing an internal market of employees and service employee job satisfaction resulting in customer satisfaction, the most recent phase in the development of internal marketing concerns the introduction of the concept of *internal market orientation* (Lings, 2004). It assumes that the effectiveness of a marketing strategy not only depends on the ability of the organisation to be responsive to the needs of its customers (termed external market orientation), but also relies on its ability to align its internal environment with its strategic marketing objectives (termed internal market orientation), to the extent that the external market orientation and an internal market orientation are symmetrical with the organisation's marketing strategy. In other words, internal and external marketing strategies need to support and reinforce each other in delivering the organisation's marketing objectives. In practical terms, internal market orientation is the company's ability to understand and respond to its service employees' needs, to make sure that they are able, equipped and motivated to deliver the type and level of service needed to support the organisation's overall strategic marketing objectives (for a further explanation, see Gounaris 2008a). This development deepens the influence of the marketing function on internal marketing.

It is recognised that internal marketing's scope, direction and outcomes are a consideration of the organisation's marketing strategy – fitting with the company's external marketing objectives and aligned with the overall strategy. Implicit in this is that the marketing function has a mandate to influence internal marketing at the strategic level and, in turn, has a stake in developing service-minded and customer-orientated employees. This, however, is where marketing's influence ends, as an internal market orientation in operational terms concerns gaining internal market intelligence (segmenting the internal market and gathering information), managing internal communication (between managers and managers and employees) and responding to market intelligence using conventional internal marketing tools of training, management concern and remuneration and so on (Gounaris, 2008b).

Marketing's influence on internal marketing and service delivery

In theory, the influence that the marketing function has on internal marketing is limited, as internal marketing concerns using 'marketing-like' thinking and activity to address the internal market of employees. The aim of this is to enhance employee job satisfaction and to influence employees' service-mindedness and customer orientation, in order to improve service quality and customer satisfaction. It is not the role of the marketing function to direct and manage all aspects of the company's internal operations that have an impact on the delivery of service quality and, consequently, customer satisfaction. Through the development of internal marketing, the marketing function operates at its margins. At best, assuming that marketing has the necessary influence within a business, the marketing function is limited to:

- Being a stakeholder and influencer
- Communicating its external marketing activity internally
- Providing advice on how marketing-like activity (i.e. segmentation and market research) can be used to address the internal market of employees effectively.
- Leaving the role of developing the capabilities, service-mindedness and customer orientation of service employees to the HR and service operations functions.

So is that where the situation is to be left? Is the role of the marketing function predominantly to concern itself with purely external commercial matters and limit its contribution internally? If this is the case, this raises the question of how, in a services environment, marketing can be expected to deliver its objectives effectively. There is certainly an expectation that the promises marketing makes to markets and customers, through its value propositions and communications, should be delivered. The problem is how this can be done, if marketing has limited direct influence on the quality of the service delivered. Surely the marketing function should have more than a stake in internal marketing, when marketers are expected to deliver against market share targets, customer satisfaction ratings and so on. At face value, it is clear that certain elements of internal marketing, such as empowerment and management support, are the domain of service and operations management. But is there a way in which marketing can build on and complement internal marketing, to influence the service-mindedness and customer orientation of service employees? Is there a way in which marketing can directly encourage service employees to become part-time marketers and to deliver customer satisfaction through enhanced service quality? The answer lies with the unique environment of service employees.

The unique environment of service employees – the influence of the corporate brand

Service employees, whether in retail, service engineer or customer service roles, find themselves in a unique position: at the point at which the internal environment of the organisation intersects and meets the market and the customer. In bridging the internal and external environments, it is easy for service employees to feel that neither aspect exists in its own right. Both merge into a single environment, where the internal and the external interact (Homburg, Wieseje & Bornemann, 2009).

Here one other related asset acts as an integrator of these two environments – the corporate brand. Service employees:

- Are an audience for branded external marketing communication campaigns
- Deliver branded services and experience customer reaction
- Assess the needs of customers against the branded services they deliver
- Work in a branded corporate environment
- Receive branded briefings concerning what is expected of them to meet company targets
- Have standards set and expectations set for how they deliver the branded service.

The corporate brand (including its sub-brands) is, to a degree, always present in the service employees' working environment, continually commu-

Inside the organisation

What the organisation stands for, its mission, its objectives, what is to be achieved. How it applies to service employees.

Brand's promise and its application to service delivery

Branded work environment, and communication of progress and achievement.

Market and the consumer

Brand communication and advertising

Customer contact and feedback

Branded service delivery

Service employees evaluate: What customers think of the brand?
• Is the brand working?
• Is it delivering the brand promise?
• Do services need to improve?

Figure 10.1 The unique branded environment of service employees

nicating signals and messages about the organisation, its mission, the products and services it delivers, the brand promises made to customers and so on. This puts service employees in a unique position to:

- Evaluate what customers think of the brand
- Judge whether the brand is working in the organisation's favour
- Identify whether the brand's service is meeting the needs of the customer
- Assess how the organisation can improve the brand's service
- Assess whether it is possible to deliver to the customer what the brand is promising.

By virtue of its natural responsibility for branding, marketing should directly stimulate a debate with service employees, encouraging them to address these points. This will inevitably move them towards starting to address the internal marketing issues of service-mindedness, customer orientation, service quality and customer satisfaction.

From corporate brand to corporate identity – a direct influencer of internal marketing

The corporate brand's influence can extend further, to become much more pervasive. For instance, training materials are typically corporately branded, as are features of HR practice ranging from job adverts to job descriptions. Also, conversations about performance between managers and service employees automatically refer to the organisation by name, along with its targets and expectations (Suvatjis & de Chernatony, 2005). The corporate brand touches and directly influences certain aspects of internal marketing. The corporate brand potentially touches and becomes a direct influence on certain parts of internal marketing. Therefore a corporate brand is not merely a device designed for customer- and market-facing purposes, it becomes an all-pervasive presence inside an organisation, which if strong enough could become the essence of the organisation itself. Such a corporate identity is defined in a number of ways where the corporate brand signifies and communicates what an organisation is, the mind, soul and voice of the organisation, and the explicit management of all the ways in which the organisation presents itself through experiences and perceptions to all its audiences.

The future of marketing's internal role

A change in thinking – marketing's future role as the integrator of service employees and customers

A strong corporate brand has significant potential influence on the successful implementation of internal marketing, it enhances communications management and it supports the management of service employees' attitudes. As marketing has a responsibility for managing the corporate brand, marketers find themselves in a powerful position to change service employees' attitudes towards greater customer consciousness and service-mindedness, by communicating and deploying the corporate brand.

Marketing has the potential to use the corporate brand to build service employee brand communities that evoke service-mindedness and customer orientation, and deliver the intended outcomes of internal marketing (higher service quality and customer satisfaction). Instead of marketers being concerned with having to justify their internal role, they should instead bring down the artificial boundaries that exist between internal and external marketing. This will enable them to focus their efforts on a more effective approach – one where no real distinction exists and where all marketing activity is geared to one aim: delivering customer satisfaction through higher service quality. To this end, in managing and using the corporate brand as an integrator of the internal and external environments, marketing should create an effective services environment for customers by establishing brand communities of committed service employees. The ultimate goal is to build a single community of customers and service employees, brought together by their common identification and strong psychological ties with the corporate brand.

Consumer brand communities – the role of social identity

Strong brands such as Harley-Davidson, Apple and Volkswagen have, over time, nurtured and built consumer brand communities, where admirers of the brand, through social interaction and relationships, develop brand loyalty and form emotional connections with the brand. Members of a brand community, by default, are members of a group. Membership of such a group contributes to an individual consumer's psychological sense of their self, who they are. To the extent that an identity is developed, a social identity results from the psychology of the causes and consequences of individuals seeing themselves, and being seen by others, as part of a social group. In simple terms, by comparing the similarities and differences between the characteristics of the group and themselves, customers measure the extent of the overlap between the two. The closer the fit between the individual and the group, the more the individual will perceive themselves as a member of that group.

In brand communities, customers develop a social identity based around self-enhancement, through a boost in individual and collective self-esteem that is related to the brand itself. Customers identify directly with the brand. This brand identification follows when the customer's self-image is a close match to the brand's image (Bagozzi & Dholakia, 2006). The more the customer's social identity with the brand community increases, the more they participate in group activities. This leads to greater involvement with the brand and the customer further incorporating the brand into their sense of self. This places the marketing function in a crucial position. In managing the corporate brand and its associated brand portfolio, marketing has the potential to optimise the strength and power of a corporate brand to build consumer loyalty and ultimately build strong consumer brand communities.

The organisational identity of service employees – the corporate brand directly influences service quality

So why is social identity relevant to the marketing function's role inside organisations? Social identity is not only a consumer phenomenon, it also occurs in the working environment, where employees psychologically identify with their work group, their division and the organisation as a whole. The psychological link between an individual and their organisation is known as organisational identity. It is a form of social identity that is the extent to which individuals define their self in terms of membership of the organisation, and where identification with an organisation partly answers the question: 'Who am I?' This matters because the company is one of the groups to which the employee belongs. Research indicates that there are strong links between organisational identity and employee performance, commitment to the organisation, employee retention and job satisfaction. Significantly, organisational identity influences job satisfaction, which is critical to ensuring that employees deliver high service quality and customer satisfaction.

It follows, then, that if the marketing function can influence the organisational identity of employees, it will have the desired impact on service quality and customer satisfaction. The more an individual identifies with an organisation, the more the organisation's values, norms and interests are incorporated into their sense of self. The opportunity for the marketing function is to use the corporate brand to communicate messages about the organisation to service employees. Using the corporate brand as a shared symbol to communicate values, beliefs, roles and behaviours will enable service-mindedness and customer orientation to become deeply embedded in employees' thinking and approach – as they are incorporated into their organisational identity.

In marketing, managing, structuring and integrating the external and internal activities associated with deploying the corporate brand, and in doing so communicating to an internal target audience of service employees, the messages that result are likely to help build a stronger identification with the organisation. During this process, individuals evaluate the similarities and differences between their own personal characteristics and those of the organisation and its corporate brand. In using the corporate brand in this way, marketing directly influences the service quality and customer satisfaction delivered by service employees. But is there a further step open for the marketing function? The corporate brand could not only be used to influence the organisational identity of service employees, it could also be used to build a strong identification with the corporate brand itself.

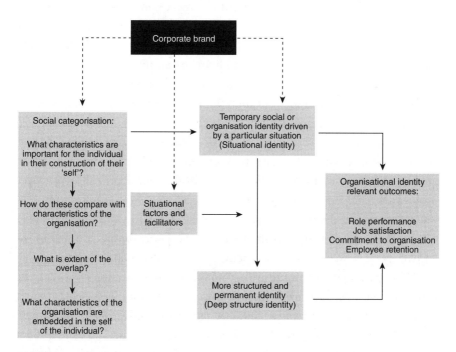

Figure 10.2 The development of an organisational identity by service employees – the potential influence of the corporate brand

Building strong service employee brand communities – a theory or a practical opportunity

Just as consumers (as members of brand communities) identify with a brand because there is an overlap with their own self-image and the brand's image, there is also the potential for service employees to identify directly with the corporate brand. As previously stated, service employees find themselves in a unique and potentially powerful position. They operate in a branded environment, receiving internal and external brand messages and signals every day. By virtue of this environment and frequent interaction with customers, they find themselves in a natural position to evaluate what customers think of the brand, to make their own evaluation of the brand and to judge whether the brand is working in the organisation's favour.

As part of their day-to-day role, service employees are not only in a position to arrive at such judgements independently, they are also in a position to discuss these issues with co-workers. It is almost inevitable that, either consciously or subconsciously, service employees will make comparisons between themselves, the features of the brand and the characteristics of the brand's operating environment. This will highlight the similarities and differences and the sense of overlap between themselves and the corporate brand. Even though such a potential identification with a corporate brand may be tacit, such a position presents a significant latent opportunity for the marketing function to open up a dialogue with service employees. By starting a debate and a series of activities, the marketing function can directly influence service quality and customer satisfaction through the development of service-mindedness and a customer orientation. Engaging service employees in this way, encouraging them to discuss and develop branding and service issues, will develop a greater identification with the corporate brand and will move employees to view themselves as members of a wider brand community.

Although a brand community may not be a formal physical entity at first, it may evolve into such over time. It is important to understand that such communities are formed and maintained psychologically through individuals identifying with the corporate brand and considering themselves as members of a wider brand community. In doing so, as part of the process of identity development, employees' individual, organisational and corporate brand identities are brought together to build a service operating environment, where service employees integrate the internal and external environments for the benefit of the customer. In developing stronger organisational and corporate brand identification, the aim is for service employees to become closely aligned with the organisation and the corporate brand and, significantly, to become strong, active brand advocates. This results in employees embodying and expressing, in their actions and behaviour, the service-mindedness and customer orientation that will deliver high service quality and customer satisfaction.

The final destination – a single corporate brand community of service employees and customers

In creating a service delivery environment that is routed to a corporate brand community, the marketing function is creating more than a climate where service-mindedness and customer orientation come as standard. With service employees developing a sense of empathy with consumers, through the

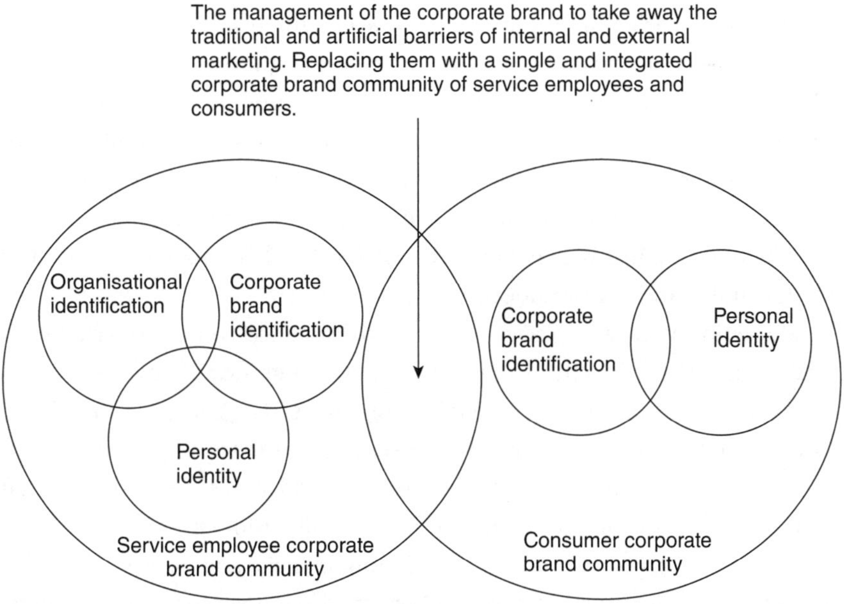

The management of the corporate brand to take away the traditional and artificial barriers of internal and external marketing. Replacing them with a single and integrated corporate brand community of service employees and consumers.

Figure 10.3 A single corporate brand community of service employees and consumers

corporate brand, marketing is integrating the organisation with its customers, bringing together service employees and customers to form a single, integrated brand community.

The journey from internal marketing to single corporate brand community

In the first instance, it appears that the marketing function's role in directly influencing and delivering the conventional configuration of internal marketing may, at best, be limited to:

- Exercising strategic influence through its inclusion within the scope of marketing strategy
- Internal briefings about marketing's external customer and market activity, to achieve awareness and commitment
- Provide advice on the implementation of 'marketing-like' activity aimed at an internal market of employees, to increase job satisfaction.

However, marketing has more than a vested interest in ensuring that the standard of service quality delivered by service employees is high, and that customer satisfaction is delivered in line with the promises and propositions it makes to customers and the market as a whole. The service-mindedness of employees and their orientation towards the customer are key concerns for marketing, as these attributes have a significant impact on the delivery targets for which marketing is generally accountable (such as market share, sales volume and brand performance).

Marketing is ideally placed not only to influence conventional internal marketing activity directly, but also to add to it significantly by influencing the attitudes and behaviours of service employees. The corporate brand and its associated brand portfolio are ever present in the service employees' operating environment, where employees form a bridge between the internal environment of the organisation and the external customer environment. In managing the corporate brand, by integrating internal and external branding activity and by targeting messages to both service employees and customers, marketing is in a position to build a single service-operating environment.

Without internal and external demarcations, this brings customers and service employees together into one brand community.

The corporate brand, in carrying messages and signals about products and services, the brand's promise and mission and so on, is not only influential in forming brand communities of customers, it also potentially influences the psychological linkage between service employees and the organisation. In carrying messages concerning service-mindedness and customer orientation, the corporate brand is prompting service employees to make comparisons between themselves and the organisation. These comparisons create a sense of how they see their 'selves' at work, resulting in a stronger organisational identity. In addition, service employees are in a unique position to evaluate the effectiveness of the corporate brand, to assess what customers think of the brand and so on. Such information is a powerful foundation for marketing to build a dialogue with service employees about service quality, delivering the brand promise and service-mindedness – with the purpose of both strengthening organisational identification and fostering a direct identification with the corporate brand itself.

Just as customer brand communities are built on brand identification, so it is possible to form brand communities of service employees based on a strong overlap between the characteristics of the corporate brand and how individual service employees see their 'selves' at work. In building communities of brand advocates, in other words part-time marketers, marketing is directly building a service-minded and customer-orientated environment that is focused on delivering service quality and customer satisfaction.

Therefore, the challenge for marketing's future internal role is to build strong service employee brand communities, populated by brand advocates (part-time marketers), with the long-term aim of integration with the organisation's customers to form a single corporate brand community.

Key questions for internal marketing

As is usually the case in writing a chapter such as this, more questions arise out of its reading than are answered in the text itself, as space

continued on next page ...

only allows for setting out general principles. For example, throughout the text only service employees and service organisations are referred to. Equally, the principles hold for organisations across the spectrum of product and service provision. Also, it has not been possible to cover more detailed material concerning the relationship between corporate brands and corporate identities – to break down the components of both and to lay out the details of how they can be integrated and communicated to build a single brand community of service employees and customers. In addition, there is more to be said about how to go about the task, given the number of brands an organisation has, their structure and their relative strength. Research surrounding the formation of identities is also valuable when contemplating the potential of the proposed approach. Further thinking and detail of how marketing engages with other constituencies in the organisation to build the debate around the commercial benefits of developing the corporate brand, and its associated portfolio, is also essential when building service employee brand communities. The recommended further reading and references go some way towards filling these gaps.

However, as a starting point, there are a series of key questions to be answered concerning your organisation's present position:

- Is internal marketing a phrase used within your organisation, and what is its popular meaning? How far does this current approach go to support the customer orientation and service-mindedness of service employees and their delivery of service quality? How much influence does, should and could the marketing function have in this domain?
- Does your organisation's marketing strategy consider the marketing department's influence on internal issues, such as the quality of service delivery and managing the internal impact of the corporate brand? What are the implications of this for the performance of the marketing function and in delivering customer satisfaction?
- Apart from standardised customer satisfaction and employee satisfaction surveys, does your organisation measure and monitor what

continued on next page ...

influences and drives both types of satisfaction and the relationship between the two? What are the current levels of service employee organisational and corporate brand identification? What are the implications for the organisation, its performance and, specifically, its brand advocacy and service quality? To what extent, explicitly or latently, might service employee brand communities exist? How closely aligned are service employees and customers?

- To what extent does your organisation take a structured approach to developing and managing both the corporate brand and its related brand portfolio? How strong are the corporate brand and portfolio? How might internal and external activity be integrated for the benefit of both service employees and customers, as well as to build brand strength? Do consumer brand communities exist for the organisation's brand portfolio, on what strengths are they formed and to what stage have they developed?

- What is the potential for engaging service employees in a debate around their experiences and perceptions of how the corporate brand (and its associated portfolio) is performing? What could be done to bring about this debate? Who are the key stakeholders, and how might this benefit them?

References and further information

Bagozzi, P.G. & Dholakia, U.M. (2006) Antecedents and purchase consequences of customer participation in small group brand communities, *International Journal of Research in Marketing*, 23: 45–61.

Berry, L.L. (1981) The employee as the customer, *Journal of Retail Banking*, 3(1): 33–40.

Gounaris, S. (2008a) The notion of internal market orientation and employee job satisfaction: Some preliminary evidence, *Journal of Services Marketing*, 22(1): 68–90.

Gounaris, S. (2008b) Antecedents of internal marketing practice: Some preliminary empirical evidence, *International Journal of Service Industry Management*, 19(3): 400–34.

Gronroos, C. (2000) *Service Management and Marketing: A Customer Relationship Management Approach*, 2nd edn, Chichester: John Wiley & Sons Ltd.

Gummesson, E. (1999) *Total Relationship Marketing*, Oxford: Butterworth-Heinemann.

Homburg, C., Wieseje, J. & Bornemann, T. (2009) Implementing the marketing concept at the employee–customer interface: The role of customer need knowledge, *Journal of Marketing*, 73: 64–81.

Lings, L.N. (2004) Internal market orientation: Constructs and consequences, *Journal of Business Research*, 57(4): 405–13.

Suvatjis, J.Y. & de Chernatony, L. (2005) Corporate Identity Modelling: A Review and Presentation of a New Multi–dimensional Model, *Journal of Marketing Management*, 21: pp. 809–834.

Chapter 11

John Grant
Author and consultant

John Grant is the author of five business books including *The Green Marketing Manifesto*. He was a former co-founder of St Luke's, the socially aware ad agency, and co-founder of Abundancy Partners, a strategic sustainability consultancy. He also operates as an independent consultant and recent clients include the BBC, Cisco, IKEA, Innocent Drinks, Microsoft and Unilever. John is also an adviser to social ventures, public bodies and charities.

In recent years it has become clear that achieving an ethical, sustainable approach to business is one of the most significant challenges ever faced by commercial enterprises. Increasingly, customers and other stakeholders value both a sustainable approach to business and one that is commercially successful. Those forward-thinking organisations that are able to achieve both are finding that the rewards are well worth the effort.

The green shoots of sustainability

Brand marketing and sustainability are often thought of as opposites. In simplistic terms, the former urges people to consume more and the latter to consume less. Creating an effective 'green marketing' that meets both aims is therefore one of the most interesting challenges in modern business (it's right up there with humanising technology and creating local authentic connections for global brands).

Yet it is far from a simple case of two entirely separate and contradictory domains. Like many cultural opposites, brands and sustainability are also intertwined. The history of their connection goes back a long way, to ancient history when both were present at (and connected to) the invention of money, arithmetic and writing. All of these, like brands, originated as marks made in clay or metal, usually as records of fair dealing by merchants or manufacturers – as *trade marks*, in other words.

Timeless attributes, universally valued: Authenticity and quality

The earliest brands are also some of the earliest records of writing. For example, the seals on storage jars (which acted as anti-tamper evidence) used symbols and very early hieroglyphs that indicated provenance and quality. The issue of authenticity and transparency, one of the key themes in this chapter, is not new. Nor is the question of ethical production, if you consider the ancient taboos and rituals surrounding food, such as the religious prescriptions about how animals are to be slaughtered. Eco-labels in their modern form resemble these seals, signifying an inspection stamp and drawing on archetypal religious images. It is interesting to note that the Fairtrade logo is yin and yang, the Organic logo is the Celtic Triskelian and the Rainforest Alliance uses a classic animal talisman. In the mid-nineteenth century some brands of sugar were sold on their 'slave labour-free' origins, the Fairtrade identity of its age. Eco-labels, in other words, are not the newest additions to the branding scene; they are some of the oldest.

> Eco-labels are not the newest additions to the branding scene – they are some of the oldest.

In a way, all brands are 'ethical and environmental labels': they are trade marks acting as a basic reassurance of a product's authenticity as well as connoting the reputable values of an organisation. The OXO stock cube literally originated as a quality inspection mark made at the Argentine docks on crates bound for the UK. And consider that at the time when America was giving rise to brands such as Coca-Cola, hygiene levels resembled those found today in Sub-Saharan Africa and food safety and integrity were real concerns. The new national brands like Coca-Cola and Kellogg's guaranteed consistent quality for an increasingly mobile workforce – people who had to trust the food and drink that were available when they were far from home.

The origins of green marketing

Marketing and ethics may be intertwined, but they have also made uneasy companions throughout their history. The image of the unscrupulous merchant – the greengrocer who hides the bruised fruit at the bottom of the bag, or the tailor who pinches the back of the coat to make it appear to fit when you try it on – are as old as marketplaces. Little wonder that *caveat emptor* remains as a phrase still widely used.

There are also deep symbolic structures – archetypal ideas – within which brands, like movies and political narratives, play out. For example, Monsanto and the protests against genetically modified (GM) food were a clear example. Whatever the material case for or against GM foods, there was a profound cultural dissonance. There is a widespread cultural concern that, if scientists tinker with nature behind closed doors, they risk creating Frankenstein's monster. And the backlash against GM foods in the UK was precisely against what the tabloids called 'Frankenstein foods'.

Conversely, the Body Shop brand under the early leadership of its founder Anita Roddick seemed to draw on the narrative arc of St Joan (even including a betrayal by her own forces). Ethical marketing is not alone in touching on such themes. But perhaps because it connects with values that people hold 'sacred', its symbolic and cultural dimensions are magnified. Ethical brands tend to be idealised as 'saintly' and can easily fall from grace should they 'sell out', for instance when acquired by a more worldly corporation.

Such a backlash happened when the Innocent drinks company conducted a small-scale trial with McDonald's in 2008. Logically there was nothing they ever said about refusing to be stocked in retail outlets that didn't share their values (for example, their products are routinely stocked in big oil companies' forecourts, but it had never been made an issue). In cultural terms, however, a liaison with McDonald's was seen as some kind of pact with the devil. No matter that in some sustainability circles McDonald's was by now felt to be one of the good guys; the previous year, it had even been named one of the '100 most ethical companies in the world' by *Ethisphere* magazine. Nevertheless, McDonald's was known by the green consumer audience more for its McLibel era and was one of the corporations that the anti-globalisation movement loved to hate. As a result, the aptly named Innocent suffered the worst sort of backlash, one within its own fan base. Close community members left hurt and hurtful messages like 'thanks for all the smoothies'.

So the current 'green marketing' boom did not entirely spring out of a vacuum. The underlying cultural and psychological structures on which it is built have a long history. In particular, some of the inherent fault lines and risks in 'greening your brand' were evident in the previous green consumer boom of the 1990s.

The green consumer bandwagon

The start of the 1990s was a special moment in time. The Berlin Wall had just fallen and there had been a decade of humanitarian disasters, perhaps most memorably brought to the public attention by Live Aid in 1985. In

1988–89 there were continuing wars and famine in Ethiopia, Sudan, Angola and Mozambique, combined with floods in Bangladesh, earthquakes in Armenia and San Francisco and a major hurricane season in the Caribbean. All of this created a widespread feeling of anxiety and concern about failing environmental systems, as well as rising concern about the depletion of the ozone layer. In 1990 the Gulf War broke out; in 1994 Rwanda experienced the fastest genocide in history; and through the 1990s there were wars in the Balkans. One consequence of these events was a time of millennial anxiety, a corresponding rush of concern about saving the planet and a cultural mood shift – what the Henley Centre has called 'the caring sharing 90s'.

Into this context was born the green consumer boom. *The Green Consumer Guide* by John Elkington and Julia Hailes, published in 1989, became a best-seller. Brands like the Body Shop and Ecover went from fringe players to mainstream high-growth stars. Major manufacturers and retailers (such as Boots with its 'Natural Collection' and Reckitt and Colman's 'Down to Earth') rushed to produce their own versions. You couldn't move in the supermarket for new-fangled claims about green products together with recycled bin bags and CFC-free sprays. At the time, this was called the green consumer band-wagon and there was what looked like an unseemly scramble to climb aboard. And it wasn't just about sales in the supermarket. The UK Green Party enjoyed a surge in popularity, winning 15 per cent of the national vote in the European elections of 1990.

There was thus a surge of interest in these 'eco-friendly' products, but only a few years later there was a backlash. Joel Makower (author of the bestselling 1990 book *The Green Consumer*) blames shoddy product quality – for example the recycled bin bags that split and the detergents that didn't get your clothes clean. Whatever the cause of the reversal, it turned into a stampede. Supermarkets

> The constant drumbeat of sustainability is now the result of rational analysis and widespread understanding. Sustainability is clearly the way the world is going, of necessity.

delisted the green products as fast as they had listed them. Reckitts dropped its eco range and 'green' dropped out of the public and political consciousness.

Interestingly, the tendency when a big issue (like environmentalism) gains prominence in the public consciousness relatively quickly is to get sucked into 'bandwagon' thinking. The issue assumes the status of a management fad. People stop asking questions about the audience and product proposition, and a magical thinking arrives that suspends critical discussion. Instead, people believe that 'if we build it, they will come'. (A similar mindset drove off rational thinking a few years later, when billions were invested in loss-making internet companies.) It is important, however, to look beyond the hype and the backlash, the hyperbole and the sceptics' dismissal. The constant drumbeat of sustainability is now the result of rational analysis and widespread understanding. Sustainability is clearly the way the world is going, of necessity. It is a new paradigm and there will be new stars. However, this makes strategic thinking about green issues vital: it is a difficult challenge to get right.

One iconic test case was Iceland Frozen Foods in 2001. There had been a big shift to organic produce – for example, more than half of the market for baby foods was organic. However, when Iceland switched to organic there was a huge backlash. Basically, it had ignored its *core proposition*, which was price, and its *audience*, which was cash-strapped young families. The same audience had willingly bought into Body Shop, one of whose key segments was young mothers, but in that case what was being offered was a killer combination of *better products* (natural ingredients, good-quality formulations and ethical sourcing) that were *much cheaper*. During this time, Body Shop founder Anita Roddick summed up its business idea as 'putting the money into the product not the packaging'. The key was using only a few packaging formats, only having a few types of bottles and tubs, meaning that they could be bought in huge bulk, as well as cutting retooling costs. This contrasted sharply with Iceland, who simply faced its value-seeking consumer with an overnight price hike. It lost 1.5 per cent of its sales overnight; within months it reversed the decision, its incoming CEO describing the move to organic as 'bold but misguided'.

Organic food is still haunted by this pricing problem. It gained hugely during the green consumer boom of the 2000s, being seen as not merely healthy and less damaging to the environment but also as a status symbol. When the recession and a new mood of thrift arrived, however, sales of organic food and sustainable products suffered – although some analysts suggested that it was not so much a perceptual problem as one of price difference.

The growth of sustainable marketing

The new wave

Integrating sustainability and marketing has been a hot topic in recent years. The *Financial Times* called this a 'Wave of Eco Marketing' (2007), and the amounts invested have been significant. For instance, General Electric spent more than $100 million on its Ecomagination campaign.

Many of my clients have been wrestling with the challenges of green marketing. Should they engage with it? If they do, will they be a hostage to fortune; if they don't, will they get left behind? My broad conclusion is that green marketing is not about making normal stuff seem 'green', it's about making green stuff seem normal. This former manoeuvre is known as *greenwash*, whereas green marketing will only succeed if it is authentic and able to offer something genuinely different and appealing.

> Green marketing is not about making normal stuff seem 'green'; it's about making green stuff seem normal.

The word 'greenwash' originated in an article in the mid-1980s about hotel towel schemes. The journalist's question was simple: it's fair enough for a hotel to ask me to use the same towel and save on the resources required to wash it every day, but what else are the hotels doing beyond asking their customers to make changes? The answer, the journalist concluded, was not very much. It was a case of greenwash (similar to whitewash, but for environmental issues), with green washing schemes perhaps being used to 'launder' the company's reputation.

The opposite approach is to use the power of your brand to broker change. This may not provide a 'quick fix' as easily as greenwashing but it is much more beneficial – in every respect the gains are greater. Using the power of a brand to effect change means that there is real substance to your activities, even if you are not perfect in every respect. For instance, by teaching people how to drive in a way that is ecologically friendly, the Ford motor company is doing something substantial and worthwhile. This is also the secret of modern marketing: to engage your audience and take them on a journey with you (literally, in the case of Ford). The modern power of brands means that today they can function as a surrogate tradition or custom. For instance, Nike was able to catch a wave of enthusiasm about jogging (this was a wave which its co-founder, Bill Bowerman, had started with a million-selling book).

Clearly, not every brand is as powerful as Nike or Ford. It also takes careful analysis to work out what change you could broker credibly that will make a substantial difference and work for your brand. But it's not exactly rocket science. For instance, recent suggestions that we made to a tea client included teaching people the benefits of not overfilling kettles, finding ways to make leaf tea fashionable again and making composting seem 'normal' to the UK public.

Another concern in this area is with the number of reports and experts who try to sell 'one true way'. My experience of working with a diversity of clients, audiences and situations is that green marketing is pretty much as diverse as digital marketing, experience marketing or any other form of marketing. Our clients are as diverse as Innocent smoothies, technology company Cisco, consumer products giant Unilever, financial company ING, furniture retailer IKEA, the UK government and many business start-ups and campaigns. The idea that all of these should have one tone of voice, one message and one audience is nonsense. This is the type of thinking that leads to endless repetitive ads (for example, a girl runs in a field wearing a hippy dress blowing a dandelion, or a polar bear pauses and looks up to blue skies – thankfully not in the same field as the girl with the dress and the dandelion). The reality is that there is a place for diverse strategies, with each one carefully planned and designed for a specific purpose. In fact, most of the 'how to communicate about climate change' reports do have a clear focus, limited scope and application.

In my 2007 book *The Green Marketing Manifesto*, I attempted to map out the diversity of approaches taken under the broad heading of 'green marketing'. There is not enough space here to cover the 18 different types of strategy, but it is worth highlighting four quite distinct approaches taken by leading green marketers.

Developing green brands

Green brands are, in general, green companies.

Clearly, it doesn't sit well to make a 'pure' range across the corridor from colleagues who are busy polluting the environment, our bodies or indeed our culture. That already tells you something about how green marketing is a little different from other topics. Most corporate marketing is based on the concept of the portfolio: offering different benefits to different audiences under different brand names. But it does not work well to have a portfolio with varying ethical standards. For example, Unilever is often criticised for having the brands Dove (real beauty) and Axe/Lynx (real sexism) under the same roof.

People do understand, however, that firms may have flagship products that are further advanced than their overall range. Many companies develop iconic products that may be ahead of other products in the same organisation or portfolio (such as Toyota's Prius), and there is a rationale in supporting their R&D efforts while also expecting a transition. Unfortunately, there are no hard-and-fast rules and this is a fast-moving issue. It was exactly this type of 'ethical spread' that got BP into trouble over its claim to be 'Beyond Petroleum'.

Green brands are also an enigma in that they almost never succeed by marketing their greenness. Ecover has spent 20 years convincing us that it can get our clothes clean. Method brought Apple-style 'cool' to worthy household cleaning products. Clothing brand Howies is also über cool (it was named above Nike in a list of the world's coolest companies). Green and Blacks created a new kind of luxury chocolate category. There are cases where green brands need to bring people into the fold – for instance, convincing people to buy green electricity. But generally, green is the underpinning for creating true brand differentiation, value and loyalty – as well as genuine relationships with real human connections.

Setting new standards

Corporate branding has probably been the main story in the last wave of eco-marketing. It's been less about recycled packaging and more about reconfigured companies.

A prime example is the Marks & Spencer (M&S) 'Plan A' campaign. As a piece of marketing, this resembles a government policy initiative more than anything a company would usually do. Other similar examples include HSBC and the Climate Partnership, the carbon-neutral and pro-behaviour change Sky/Newscorp, the Virgin War Room, the Together consortium and GE's Ecomagination.

The truth is that creating a sustainable economy requires large-scale rethinking of supply chains, business models and markets. It is (to paraphrase what Accenture used to say about digital) the new strategy. Unilever's recently announced company vision is a typical example. What is really extraordinary is that this is not a sustainability vision; it is a *whole company* vision:

> We work to create a better future every day.
>
> We help people feel good, look good and get more out of life with brands and services that are good for them and good for others.
>
> We will inspire people to take small everyday actions that can add up to a big difference for the world.
>
> We will develop new ways of doing business that will allow us to double the size of our company while reducing our environmental impact.

The evidence is clear: those companies that take a lead on sustainability issues thrive. Successful businesses such as M&S can point to millions of pounds of additional profits generated by Plan A and it is not difficult to understand why. Sustainable business can protect against risk, reduce costs, spur innovation and enhance reputation. These benefits lie behind the wave of corporate green advertising, which, perhaps mysteriously, does work – perhaps because questions of trust and integrity are so significant for all those marginal decisions about what mortgages to consider or where to refuel your car. It might be that the bigger theme is a shift from buying brands to seeing the producers behind them. That was certainly the theory put forward to explain the first wave of green companies in the 1990s, such as Benetton and Body Shop. The choice of company is becoming a question of shared political values rather than image.

'Doing our bit'

Another significant approach used by green marketers is that we should 'all do our bit' and take little actions to reduce waste and improve sustainability. This is the most direct application of the idea that good green marketing can change the way people think and behave. The standout example has been Ariel's 'Turn to 30', where the firm encouraged people to turn their washing machines down so that they washed at 30°C. This action was cited in a 2008 survey by IPC magazines as the main new thing that consumers had done in response to their concerns about climate change.

The 'little actions' approach has been controversial. Some people criticise it because of *cultural dissonance*. The argument goes that it is not credible that we can avert a global apocalypse by changing light bulbs or unplugging phone chargers. Other criticisms include the claim that the gains lead to a larger *systemic self-deception* where, by feeling we have 'done our bit', we rebound into other behaviours that are just as harmful.

> Achieving a change in behaviour is a particularly challenging but significant and substantial aspect of green marketing.

It strikes me that behaviour change is a particularly challenging but successful and substantial aspect of green marketing. For example, the gains made in teaching people eco-driving can match those that take decades in car engineering terms. These, in turn, pale into insignificance if you can get people to change habits and car share, use a car club, turn a journey into a videophone meeting and so on. Green marketing is a way to take people on a journey towards a better quality of life and, crucially, one that they have freely chosen.

Developing new models and markets: Green 2.0

This is my particular area of focus: developing new models and markets on cooperative rather than narrow, selfish or individualist lines. Cooperation in games theory means acting for the benefit of the whole group rather than individuals. This is also the best way to preserve one's own interests too, particularly in times of crisis. 'Everyone for themselves' is the most dangerous approach to a fire exit for all involved.

Developing new approaches is where marketing blends innovation with business strategy. The general challenge is to create maximum well-being for the minimum amount of resources and impact, a priority that is clearly expressed in Unilever's vision. This is the way in which ecosystems work, optimising their life-support functions with surprising degrees of cooperation within and between species (surprising compared with the neo-classical view of survival of the fittest).

I have written a book surveying the main developments in green 2.0 (*Co-opportunity*). Some of the typical approaches include:

- *Crowd funding* – this ranges from well-meaning donations to a strategic engagement platform (this was particularly successful during the 2008 US Presidential election).
- *Purchase-power aggregation* – this can work at a wide range of levels, from community-supported agriculture (with local people buying local produce) to community-choice aggregation (whole cities buying green energy cheaply).
- *Dynamic demand* – this is a great example of green 2.0 resulting in innovation and improvements, and it is highlighted by initiatives such as smart city grids, flexible public transport routing or using energy at times of spare grid capacity.
- *Sharing and collaborative consumption* – a great example of this approach is the adoption of flexible 'pay per use' pricing covering everything from vehicles to handbag rental.
- *Social production* – in this model much of the value is created by 'consumers', for example in the form of reviews on Amazon.com and other user-generated content, co-creation and open innovation.

The future for sustainable marketing

It seems likely that the key development for sustainable marketing in the next ten years could be the 95 per cent of organisations catching up with the 5 per cent who have already taken the lead. In other words, as with the internet and ecommerce, sustainable marketing will become routine and ubiquitous instead of exceptional or unusual.

However, there are signs of yet more disruptive change heading our way too. The consequences of a decade that included a credit crunch, food crisis, oil price spikes and other global developments suggest that the future may be neither smooth nor predictable but volatile, fast-moving and different.

Another key theme may also be present alongside this volatility: a transition from choice to necessity, with, for instance, a permanent shift in who pays the cost of dirty operations. One development that fascinates me is the potential for far greater transparency and democracy within consumer markets. We do, after all, live in the information age. The Wal-Mart Index is one initiative among several that points towards a time where, rather than leaving it to brands to tell us, we will simply know what a product contains, how it was produced and how it fits with our values. The growth of *intermediation* – a situation where intermediaries put valuable information in the public domain – means that while we may not individually have the time and inclination to explore every purchase in depth, others will do this for us.

Predicting the future is never wise, especially in print, but my exposure to the scientists, policy makers and campaigners driving the sustainability agendas leads me to suspect that we could well see more change in the next 20 years than in the last 200. After all, it's worth remembering that while change is difficult, messy and risky for larger organisations, for marketers and innovators it will continue to drive what we do.

Key questions about sustainability

- Is your organisation serious about being an environmentally responsible business? In particular, do you and your colleagues genuinely value the benefits of a sustainable approach to business, or are you at risk of simply trying to *appear* green?

continued on next page ...

- What are the risks, benefits and opportunities of being green? What are the implications for your products and services, customers, sales, costs and people?
- How can you quickly develop your position as a green business – where are the best opportunities and quick wins (the 'low-hanging fruit')?
- What opportunities are there to disrupt your industry and clearly distinguish your business from your competitors using green marketing?
- Which elements of your business should be reviewed and revised if your values, focus and approach become genuinely green? For example, should you reconsider your vision, product range, pricing model, market segments – or something else?
- How can you improve your products or service with a greener approach (for example by encouraging sharing and collaborative consumption or social production)?
- What can you learn from other organisations, sectors and countries?

References and further information

Epstein, M.J. (2008) *Making Sustainability Work: Best Practices in Managing and Measuring Corporate Social, Environmental and Economic Impacts*, Sheffield: Greenleaf Publishing.

Esty, D. & Winston, A. (2009) *Green to Gold: How Smart Companies Use Environmental Strategy to Innovate, Create Value, and Build Competitive Advantage*, Chichester: John Wiley & Sons Ltd.

Grant, J. (2007) *The Green Marketing Manifesto*, Chichester: John Wiley & Sons Ltd.

Grant, J. (2010) *Co-opportunity: Join Up for a Sustainable, Resilient, Prosperous World*, Chichester: John Wiley & Sons Ltd.

Laszlo, C. (2008) *Sustainable Value: How The World's Leading Companies Are Doing Well by Doing Good*, Sheffield: Greenleaf Publishing.

Savitz, A.W. (2006) *The Triple Bottom Line: How Today's Best-run Companies Are Achieving Economic, Social and Environmental Success – And How You Can Too*, San Francisco, CA: Jossey Bass.

Chapter 12

Veronica Sharp
Director, The Social Marketing Practice

Veronica Sharp is a highly-experienced social marketer and Director of The Social Marketing Practice. She specialises in behaviour change through applied social marketing, with emphasis on policy, sustainable market development and lifestyle trends. She is also the Chair of The Chartered Institute of Marketing's specialised Member Interest Group (MIG) for Social Marketing. The group welcomes all marketers who work in or are interested in social marketing.

Social marketing is a powerful way to change people's behaviour for the benefit of society. It is defined as 'the systematic application of marketing, alongside other concepts and techniques, to achieve specific behavioural goals for a social and environmental good'. In practice, it involves tackling some of society's most challenging problems by changing the behaviour and attitudes of individuals – no small task.

Right from the start: The growth of social marketing

The origins of social marketing can be seen in any social (or societal) marketing issue where voluntary action or change was required. The concept of 'marketing for good' has developed since the 1960s and is used by governments today to address a range of issues including smoking, sexual health, blood donation, community development, obesity and climate change. Social marketing arose because of the need to achieve substantial and permanent changes in the way people live. These 'intervention' campaigns gave rise to the concept of 'social marketing' – a term first used by Philip Kotler.

In the UK, we have learnt much from the past and from international experience. We have moved on from telling people what to do (or, more accurately, urging and warning them) to tackling the much more sophisticated challenge of influencing and sustaining behavioural change. Social marketing has developed in the UK to such an extent that it is now embedded in our policy and delivery frameworks; and in 2009, social marketing was formally acknowledged through a distinct set of occupational standards – a world first!

Understanding social marketing

The *'THINK!'* Road Safety campaign, launched in 2000 as part of the UK government's strategy to cut the number of deaths and serious injuries from road accidents, has developed and strengthened over time. *THINK!* is about saving lives and it campaigns all year round to get people to think more about road safety, whether walking, driving or riding a motorcycle. The strategy set targets to reduce road casualties in Great Britain by 50 per cent for children and 40 per cent overall between 2000 and 2010. It uses a combination of enforcement, education measures, partnerships and campaigning to help meet its targets. Speed remains one of the biggest contributory factors in fatal road accidents. In 2008, 4685 people were killed or seriously injured in crashes where a speed contributory factor was reported (RCGB, 2008).

> Social marketing has grown during the twenty-first century, driven by concerns about a range of social issues.

THINK! has seen some improvements in speeding behaviours. In 1995 72 per cent of cars exceeded the speed limit on 30 mph roads; by 2005 this had reduced to 49 per cent. *THINK!* is largely effective for two reasons: it understands not just *what* people are doing but *why* they are doing it; and its power is fostered through an attitude of shared responsibility on which it targets potent messages at specific segments.

Another example of the impact of social marketing is shown by the campaign run from 2002 to 2006 by the US Department of Health and Human Services' Center for Disease Control and Prevention. With the slogan 'It's What You Do', this campaign 'for-kids-by-kids' aimed to increase and maintain physical activity among 'tweens' (children aged 9–13). After one year the campaign achieved a 32 per cent decline in the number of sedentary 9–10 year olds, and a 38 per cent decline in sedentary children from low-income groups. The strength of the campaign lay in its comprehensive research that informed the marketing strategy. By analys-

> The strength of social marketing lies in understanding the person as an individual and as a member of a community and then setting them within the wider context of the social, environmental and political influences in which they live. This total approach provides a means of achieving positive and sustainable change, leading to a better society.

ing and addressing the issues from many perspectives (from the influence of societal pressures and group dynamics to the impact of branding and different marketing messages), a social marketing campaign was developed that was capable of effecting a change in behaviour among children and sustaining that change.

There are several reasons social marketing is so distinctive. At its heart is the need to focus on behaviour and generate genuine insight and understanding. It is a process of continuous learning and measurement. All of these elements are, of course, also present in commercial marketing.

Having drawn from commercial marketing and since trodden a separate path, social marketing has emerged as a distinct marketing discipline. However, while there are cultural – and even ethical – differences, there is a good deal of common ground. Many of the principles of marketing (such as segmentation, planning and measurement) are consistent and present in both social marketing and commercial marketing, and that neither is about philanthropy or cause-related marketing.

We both seek success: commercial marketers measure success in terms of financial profit; while social marketers measure those who have taken action and experienced benefits *because* of the action. The latter is challenging and often difficult to attribute directly or wholly to the intervention.

We both focus on the customer: beginning with in-depth insight, to understand and reduce the barriers, we aim to make the benefits so appealing that people won't mind overcoming the barriers. Commercial marketers do this by changing their pricing plans, package design and distribution. Social marketers do this by tapping into motivations beyond the behaviour itself (for example by reinforcing the health benefits of walking or cycling instead of using the car to reduce carbon emissions).

We both focus on the competition: however, social and commercial marketers often compete for the same share of spend. These competing forces are extremely challenging for social marketers, particularly where commercial marketers are offering counter-productive products (for example reducing obesity when there continues to be high sugar and fat content in foods).

We both focus on behaviour: however, social marketers often work with people whose behaviour is the hardest of all to change – for example those who are disadvantaged, hard to reach or socially excluded and who face huge social, cultural and peer pressures, creating barriers and resistance to change. Behaviours are also much more complex, usually engrained in deep-seated habits that are hard to break, have limited personal value, or require substantial changes to infrastructure – such as using public transport instead of the car.

We both work with stakeholders: changing behaviours requires the involvement of a wide community of stakeholders. However, the nature of the relationships varies. For commercial marketers it is important that they are aligned to the brand, product or service delivery; for social marketers there is a complex web of relationships requiring several partners and intermediaries to *sign up* to common objectives and provide a *trusted* voice. Building these relationships is challenging and time consuming and can run the risk of messages being diluted or misrepresented.

A new challenge for social marketing

Increasing legislation and government targets require businesses to take an active role in supporting and influencing the social and environmental challenges set out by government policy. Lessening the impact of climate change, driving down crime, reducing inequalities, encouraging healthy lifestyles and improving social justice are some of the key policy drivers with which businesses, especially marketers, should become engaged. Moreover, there is a growing expectation from the public that business should take an active and responsible role in social and environmental stewardship.

Government, business and consumers occupy different corners in a dynamic 'triangle of change' (Figure 12.1). While no one, or even two groups, can lead alone, they need a coordinated and collective approach to change. While government is best placed to provide an enabling policy framework, business has a vital and responsible role in supporting and delivering change, and so do consumers in taking personal responsibility for their actions.

In the past there has been reluctance by the public sector to engage directly in partnerships with the private sector to achieve common aims. This is not surprising since, for example, marketers were fast to take advantage of the ethical shift in consumer values – exploiting 'ethics' as a selling point or a component of corporate image. Actions like this led to companies masquerading behind 'greenwash' (see Chapter 11). This, and many similar actions, put into question the ethical principles and values of commercial marketing. With

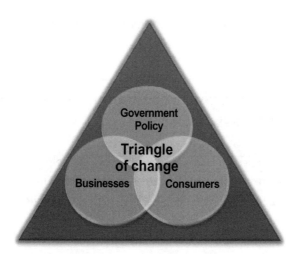

Figure 12.1 The triangle of change

the increasing need for the private sector to become actively involved in social change, trust in the ethical values of a commercial brand is crucial. While the moral principles of commercial marketing continue to be debated, the growth in 'corporate responsibility' may provide a point of connection between commercial and social marketers. However, transparency, accountability and responsibility need to be actively demonstrated – the bedrock of corporate responsibility.

The potential for collaborative approaches between the private sector on the one hand, and the public and voluntary sectors on the other, has not yet been widely exploited. A number of good examples do exist, but they are in the minority and not yet the norm. However, while commercial marketing continues to suffer from negative associations and struggles for respectability, should social marketing be used as a differentiator for economic gain? Would the credibility of social marketing be diminished if it is utilised mainstream by commercial marketers? Does social marketing run the risk of being abused? These are challenging questions for social marketers, many of whom are divided on the issue.

Working together inevitably presents challenges, including cultural and ethical differences, but there are significant opportunities to be gained in sharing skills, and aligning products and services to deliver more coherent and targeted social and environmental goals.

Taking on the toughest challenges: The social marketing process

Given the significance and complexity of social marketing, it is valuable to understand what it involves and how to ensure success. The social marketing process is comprehensive, detailed and proven and it includes several stages (Figure 12.2):

- Scoping
- Planning
- Piloting
- Implementing
- Monitoring and evaluating.

This process provides a practical way to ensure that social marketing succeeds.

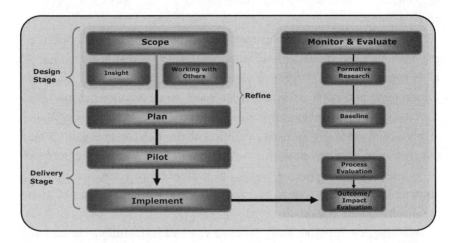

Figure 12.2 The Social Marketing Process (adapted by The Social Marketing Practice)

Scoping

Social marketing starts with defining a behavioural goal: what behaviour do you want to change? Whose behaviour do you want to change? This 'pre-scoping' exercise should aim to establish your behaviour goal, identify targets and define the desired outcome of change. The key elements are: Does the goal address an existing behaviour; does it seek to maintain and support behaviour change over a sustained period; does it include preventative measures (to avoid others taking up the behaviour)? Defining a behavioural goal is an iterative process and it may be necessary to refine the goal as the scoping process develops.

A key aim of scoping is to gain a deep understanding of where people are, rather than where you think they are, might or should be. This comes from using preliminary desk and primary research to understand the range of influences, motivations and barriers to change. At the heart of this approach is the need to probe deeper into the issues involved. This reveals the key strengths, any weaknesses that need to be addressed and any necessary changes to services or operations that may be needed. Several questions are significant:

- What are the barriers to change?
- What is the motivation to change?
- What are the things that the person needs to move away from?
- What are the things that they need to move towards?
- What does the person think, feel and believe?
- Who does the person listen to and whom do they trust?

These questions help to frame the challenge. This is not a simple, superficial or easy task; it requires a mix of research techniques, such as surveys, focus groups and observations, to probe in a way that helps you to evaluate and understand deep-seated barriers and motivations to change. Crucially, this work will inform your planning stage and provide an important baseline against which to monitor changes in behaviour and outcomes.

Scoping also enables you to understand the trade-offs or the 'exchange' process – what do I have to give up (for example time, effort, convenience, social status)? What will I get instead (for example self-confidence, improved well-being, more control over my life)? It also helps determine the 'competition' in terms of what pulls the person towards the negative

> The purpose of scoping is, above all, to find ways to support behavioural change. This means that individuals and issues should not simply be viewed in isolation – scoping the range of influences is essential.

behaviour, for example peer pressure, religious beliefs, commercial advertising and marketing. These processes are essential elements of successful social marketing.

Other vital aspects of scoping include identifying which social theories to use. The use of applied social theory helps to understand how to reach people and address their specific needs. A suitable theory depends on the nature of the barriers, your target audience's needs and where and how they like to be influenced. Understanding human behaviour is a very complex area and theories are numerous. The COI document on communications and behaviour change (http://coi.gov.uk/aboutcoi.php?page=328) provides a five-step framework that shows how behavioural theory can help to define the role for communications.

Social marketing cannot operate in a vacuum. When scoping, it is important to map out all of the stakeholders influencing an individual, prioritise the influence of each stakeholder, and understand the importance of each role. Who is able to contribute to the change process? This matters, because social marketing may target a range of stakeholders, not only the people or group whose behaviour is being targeted. For example, in a campaign targeting under-age drinking, it makes sense to involve parents and bar owners, as well as directly targeting the people whose behaviour you want to change.

There are many examples of social marketing campaigns in the public sector, but some commercial organisations are also beginning to recognise the potential offered by social marketing. For example, cosmetics firm Dove used social marketing methods to alter its approach and appeal. In 2005, Dove commissioned a global study, 'Beyond Stereotypes: Rebuilding the Foundation of Beauty Beliefs', to explore what beauty means to women today. Dove's comprehensive research revealed the psychological and sociological influences that needed to be considered in order to devise an effective campaign.

In particular, its research discovered that 77 per cent of 11–14-year-olds felt fat, ugly and depressed (see CIM, 2009). This encouraged Dove to take a radically new approach.

The Dove 'Campaign for Real Beauty' is a global effort that is intended to serve as a starting point for societal change and act as a catalyst for widening the definition and discussion of beauty. The campaign supports the Dove mission: 'to make women feel more beautiful every day by challenging today's stereotypical view of beauty and inspiring women to take great care of themselves.' In addition to changing women's view of their bodies, Dove also aims to change the beauty market.

By getting to know what women really wanted in their lives, what really mattered to them, Dove devised a campaign that was built on the premise of empowering women, rather than the traditional campaign of promising superficial 'good looks'. By improving their understanding of how women perceived themselves, Dove was able to develop the right products and market them effectively. From its research, it knew which messages would work.

> Social marketing succeeds by enabling people to change, engaging with them, leading by example and providing encouragement and incentives.

Far from being a ruthless, exploitative tactic, it was a deliberative, two-way dialogue. It was a chance to give people what they were really looking for. The result was nothing less than spectacular: a 700 per cent increase in sales. And this is the power of social marketing: it gets under the skin of customers; it gets to know how they think and what motivates them; it knows exactly how to influence their behaviour and choices; and it improves society.

Dove's campaign was widely regarded as a successful attempt to show that beauty can come in a wide range of types, not simply standardised media images. However, it is not without controversy: sceptics accuse Dove of cashing in by commoditising social values and undermining the very goals that it seeks to achieve. Others say that it is up to big brands and companies to raise such important problems and engage people to fight for change. This ethical paradox clearly illustrates the point made earlier: Should social marketing be used as a differentiator for economic gain?

Planning your strategy

The benefit of scoping is that it leads to insight and in-depth understanding, and this informs the next stage of the social marketing process (and the second part of the design phase): planning your strategy. Planning your strategy has three key elements: prioritising different segments; designing the behaviour change programme through *enabling, engaging, exemplifying* and *encouraging*; and preparing for monitoring and evaluation.

Segmentation is a science and an art. It helps you to understand people who have similar needs or interests by differentiating between groups. Used extensively in commercial marketing, it is now used by the public sector – moving away from the idea that 'one size fits all'. Segmentation is based on deep consumer insight gathered during the scoping phase. The aim is to build a comprehensive 'people picture' and translate insight into a targeted and engaging marketing strategy. Its importance is in helping to satisfy the different motivations and barriers of each segment. The components of segmentation are important and should provide a mix of variables that help to identify specific groups. These should include a mix of socio-economic and geo-demographic data to derive who and where people are (for example employment, social status, where people live); behaviour to determine what people do, where and when they do it and how often (for example usage and frequency); and psychographics, which aims to tell you why people think and feel the way they do (for example attitudes, motivations, values and beliefs).

A segmentation model will provide a 'snapshot in time' – a tool to understand where your target audience is *at the current time*. Using this information as a *baseline* should provide continuous learning, revising and refining the model's initial assumptions.

The Defra environmental segmentation model divides the public into seven segments, each with a distinct set of attitudes and beliefs towards the environment. The model is used to assess the potential for further sustainable behaviours and to inform the types of interventions that are likely to be more effective with specific segments across the range of key consumption clusters, including sustainable food behaviours. More information on the segmentation model and summary profiles can be found in Defra's 'Pro-environmental Behaviours Framework' report and annexes (www.defra.gov.uk/evidence/ social/behaviour).

The development of a segmentation model should not be taken lightly; it can be a time-consuming and expensive process. Social marketers should first seek to identify whether there are suitable existing models, or whether an existing model can be adapted. An eight-step process on segmentation has been developed by the Cabinet Office (see www.cse.cabinetoffice.gov.uk/ getDynamicContentAreaSection.do?id=1 for further details).

Known as the 'Diamond Model of Behaviour Change', this approach was shaped by the UK's Department for Environment, Food and Rural Affairs (DEFRA) as a way of thinking about influencing behaviour. It ensures that all of the factors that are necessary to change behaviour are present in a success-ful campaign.

Adapted to provide a *framework for strategy development*, the 4Es model (*enabling, engaging, exemplifying* and *encouraging*) is used to design a balanced

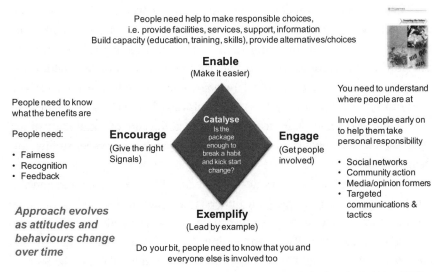

Figure 12.3 The Defra 4Es Framework (adapted by The Social Marketing Practice)

portfolio of complementary interventions and campaign activities. The appropriate mix will depend on the analysis and outcomes from the scoping phase. More than one model may be needed; that is, one for each segment or for each behaviour (if addressing more than one).

Enabling is the first stage and the priority is to make it easy for people to change by providing them with relevant help and support. For example, they need information, services and support so that they can make responsible choices. Barriers to changing need to be removed; different, attractive alternatives may need to be offered; and, where relevant, people may need to receive the relevant skills and education to change.

In some instances enabling and engaging people – making life easier for them to make the right decision – might be all that is needed. Kerbside recycling is a good example of this, a situation where providing a convenient and accessible service supported by good communications has raised recycling levels to around 39 per cent (from 14 per cent in 2001). Although attitudes have changed, there is still much to do in the UK compared to other European countries.

Engaging or getting people actively involved and 'on board' is the next challenge. Remote, 'top-down' messages from government, charities or other authorities are not enough; people need to take responsibility and act in a new way, and this requires their active engagement. Governments can provide the opportunity to recycle, save energy or improve health care, but people need to take personal responsibility for reducing their carbon footprint or living a healthy lifestyle if a lasting benefit is to be achieved. This is one of the most significant challenges at the core of social marketing: How do you get people to become engaged and take responsibility for their actions?

Think of the Chinese proverb: 'Tell me and I'll forget, show me and I'll remember ... involve me and I'll understand.' The answer lies in two-way communication, face-to-face discussion and especially the notion of *co-production or co-design*. This process involves your target audience in the process of change – right at the beginning – which not only helps to deepen your understanding but also begins to build trust and influence. It works by giving people a voice in the product or service that is being developed and it relies on mutual trust, understanding and support.

Key concept

Exemplifying social marketing

For social marketing to take root in organisations and succeed, it can't simply be 'grafted on' as an after-thought or whenever it seems most useful. Instead, it needs to become embedded in the business or organisation. This is achieved by:

- Undertaking a complete audit of existing activities – for example the organisation's supply chain.
- Providing strong, influential leadership. Crucially, this needs to explain and support the full range of social benefits, as well as explaining what needs to change.
- Managing expectations and avoiding complacency. Social marketing requires careful, diligent work as well as time to build trusted relationships and mutual understanding. In a fast-paced business culture this can be hard to maintain.

Ultimately, social marketing is about building a strong brand and an emotional connection with your audience. This is about building relationships rather than logos and strap lines. In this sense, social marketing has a deep connection with relationship marketing – building trust and deep engagement with your audience in order to encourage change.

Encouragement is another vital element of behavioural change and it involves understanding the barriers and motivations of the 'exchange': incentives to encourage the positive behaviour (for example 'buy one get one free later', in a bid by Tesco to cut food waste, means that its customers won't miss out on a free deal); and putting in place barriers to discourage behaviour (for example local authorities providing bi-weekly collections for household rubbish encourages a reduction in household waste to landfill).

Exemplifying and leading by example are crucial. The concept of 'I will if you will' (see Sustainable Development Commission, www.sd-commission.

org.uk/file_download.php?target=/publications/downloads/I_Will_If_You_
Will.pdf) clearly illustrates that people in authority need to set an example.
Fundamentally, exemplifying aims to 'put your own house in order' to ensure
that the whole process of change is not undermined by charges of hypocrisy
or a lack of credibility. For example, when UK retailer Marks & Spencer
wanted to improve its environmental management with the 'Plan A' campaign, one of its first steps was to reduce its own carbon footprint and find
ways to make improvements in its own business, before asking others to
make changes.

Monitoring and evaluating change is a crucial part of social marketing. If
you don't measure it, you can't manage it! Monitoring progress keeps your
finger on the pulse – it helps you to understand what is happening. More
specifically, it will help you to understand your target audience better, follow
their progress and determine 'customer' satisfaction; reduce risk by alerting
you early on to activities that may not be working effectively; identify measures to improve your strategy and implementation to maximise impact and
success; understand the difference that your strategy is making and to what
the difference is attributable; provide feedback to your target audience on their
progress (which is a proven incentive); and provide feedback to the project
team for learning and innovation.

Monitoring and evaluation rely on setting a baseline of attitudes and
behaviours. The baseline is developed during the scoping phase. Once set, a
series of SMART (specific, measurable, achievable, realistic and timed) objectives and key performance indicators are used to measure progress. These
will provide a reference point on which monitoring progress towards achievement of objectives can take place at discrete points in the delivery. Careful
monitoring of key performance indicators can act as an 'early warning' system,
alerting you to what might not be going as well as it should – enabling early
action.

Quantitative and qualitative data collection and evaluation methods will
be needed to monitor progress and conduct impact evaluation. For example,
a mix of surveys, focus groups, feedback sheets and participant diaries can be
used to record progress, while impact evaluation will be required to demonstrate the outcomes of your strategy to your funders and stakeholders. They
will want to know the number of people who have changed, who has changed

and sustained the change, and who has benefited as a result. They will also want you to justify a 'return on investment' that quantifies the ratio of cost savings (derived from taking action) to the cost of providing the social marketing intervention and communications. Understanding the unintended consequences and mitigating factors is also an important evaluation consideration.

Piloting

Piloting is an essential aspect of social marketing – not only does it help build momentum, it also ensures that refinements to the process can be made. For example, this stage might show that a catalyst is needed to start the process of behaviour change and help overcome deeply entrenched behaviours. The 'Eat Seasonably' campaign pilot (www.eatseasonably.co.uk) found that it needed the 'Grow Your Own' movement to help move the issue of seasonal food from the food pages to the news pages. The full campaign was launched in 2010, and has over 100 partners including pubs, restaurants, cafés, canteens and shops up and down the country who are getting involved and encouraging their customers to enjoy eating seasonably.

Piloting your strategy is important, as it allows you to assess your approach before it fully launches. Specific amendments and adjustments can then be made depending on the findings of the pilot. This increases the chances of your strategy being a success. Piloting will largely be qualitative, using tools such as focus groups or surveys to gather response attitudes and opinions on various elements of your strategy. Piloting should focus on where there is uncertainty over how your audience might respond. Above all, piloting recognises that social marketing is a dynamic process of learning and refining.

Implementing

The next stage of the social marketing process is *implementation*. During this stage it can help to ask:

- What capabilities do we have, and what skills and experience do we need to fill the gaps?

- What is the schedule of activities and tasks, and what do we have to deliver and when?
- What resources do we need in order to meet the deadlines?
- Who will be responsible for the different activities, and what will they need in order to achieve their tasks?
- What systems, standards and procedures will we need for project management, managing data, monitoring progress, recording and reporting (to time and to budget)?
- What budget do we have and what contingency plans do we have in place?
- What are our requirements for commissioning and tendering to deliver and monitor our implementation plan?
- What could go wrong, and how can we overcome possible difficulties?

This series of questions reveals what will be needed to implement the social marketing plan. Several issues need to be kept in mind at this stage. In particular, have you:

- Clearly defined the targets and outcomes of your behaviour goal? Does everyone understand them?
- Clearly defined your target audience and designed your strategy to overcome the specific barriers to change? Are the measures for providing incentives and disincentives in place?
- Put in place the intervention services, products or support that will be needed, retained or enhanced?
- Started the process of working with stakeholders (partners and intermediaries)? What type of support do they need to engage your target audience? Are your stakeholders trusted? Do they share the same goals and objectives?
- Defined the specific marketing communications mix needed to encourage your target audience?
- Commissioned external support, using experienced suppliers, where this is needed?
- Put in place policies that will exemplify and demonstrate your own commitment and advocacy?
- Made sure that the individual components of your strategy can be measured effectively and put the processes for measurement in place? How

will you ensure that feedback is provided to your target audience on their progress?

- Put in place an exit plan that leads to people taking ownership and an active role in their own well-being and that of wider society?
- Identified and addressed any 'ethical' constraints, for example around segmentation, messages and targeting, inequality etc.?

The skills of social marketing

Social marketing uses psychological, social and behavioural theories to change behaviour and encourage positive ways of living. No one person has *all* the necessary skills and experience to do social marketing by themselves! To be an effective social marketer, you need to be a good project manager and team leader, with the ability to bring together a dynamic mix of skills, expertise and tools. Research, theory, segmentation, managing stakeholder relationships, managing budgets and monitoring are all vital aspects of social marketing. Insight is your *intelligent friend*, evaluation your *critical friend*. It is important to understand your own skills – your strengths and weaknesses – and to seek to fill in the gaps.

Social marketing in the UK has developed into a distinct set of occupational marketing standards. The Social Marketing Functional Map was developed by the Marketing and Sales Standards Setting Body (MSSSB), a body recognised by the UK government as being responsible for developing UK National Occupational Standards in Marketing and Sales. The MSSSB is responsible for developing National Occupational Standards for Social Marketing. For further information, visit www.msssb.org; to see the standards, visit www.ukstandards.org/Find_Occupational_Standards.aspx?NosFindID=4&SuiteID=789.

The functions that are central to social marketing include:

- Conducting social marketing research
- Establishing and evaluating social marketing strategies
- Managing social marketing activities
- Delivering social marketing interventions
- Promoting and continuously improving social marketing.

Social marketing research

This means collecting data about the attitudes and behaviours of target groups and then developing theories about what might influence the behaviour of these groups. This informs your strategy and helps increase your understanding of the different segments within the target groups. This requires specialist skills in research and evaluation using a range of research methods.

Establishing and evaluating social marketing strategies

This allows the social marketer to develop propositions and test their ability to influence the behaviour of individuals within each target group.

Managing social marketing activities

This involves project management, managing communications, finances and people. It also includes developing networks and working with suppliers and other organisations to achieve social marketing objectives.

Delivering social marketing interventions

This is where the change is encouraged and the difference is made. It involves engaging with individuals, communities and organisations; influencing policy and decision makers; providing products or services that encourage people to adopt beneficial behaviour; providing two-way communication; and reviewing and changing systems and structures. This area includes identifying and developing relationships with stakeholders, as well as establishing and refining action plans.

Promoting and continuously improving social marketing

This is the final part of social marketing and reflects marketers' emphasis on learning and continuous improvement. It includes the need to review the results of social marketing activities, to understand their implications and share best practice, to promote a wider understanding of the benefits of social marketing (particularly among policy makers) and to provide learning products, tools, training, education and support for social marketing.

The future: The impact of social marketing

Social marketing is continuing to expand, and is increasing in popularity, understanding and effectiveness. The principles of social marketing are rigorous, insightful and beneficial. To be effective, social marketers have adopted many new skills and knowledge from other disciplines such as marketing and social psychology. If the source of social marketing can be traced to commercial marketing, then the future will see techniques and insights flowing in the opposite direction.

Social marketing is increasingly delivered by public/private partnerships that are gaining in popularity worldwide. The benefits of business, government and the not-for-profit sectors working together are compelling. There are, however, several barriers still to be overcome.

There is a lingering suspicion in society of social marketing – particularly when it is embraced by business. Developing trust is therefore a major challenge. The solution can be simple: social marketers, including businesses, have to be genuine and transparent in their motives.

Social marketing is a valuable force for good; unquestionably, it will enhance the success of purely commercial ventures. Perhaps most significantly of all, social marketing can help enhance the reputation of the marketing profession, overcoming suspicions that marketing and commerce are untrustworthy, manipulative or self-serving. However, it is interesting to note that current suspicion about social marketing is born out of the use of the word 'marketing' itself.

Key concept

The lessons of social marketing

Commercial marketers can benefit in several valuable ways by understanding the principles of social marketing. These include:

- *Developing a complete, insightful view of the customer.* Social marketers undertake in-depth research, giving them unique insights and a more

continued on next page ...

---

complete understanding of their customers, without over-emphasising a single element or feature.

- *Focusing on behaviour.* Social marketers recognise the need to change the way people behave – difficult to achieve but immensely valuable. Persuading the customer that it is in their interests to change can only be done with a gradual process that emphasises mutual understanding.
- *Adopting a patient, long-term perspective.* Achieving changes in behaviour is neither simple nor especially quick. It is a long-term process that involves continuous learning, the development of trusted relationships and the ability to provide an appealing offer.
- *Working closely with stakeholders to co-design,* together with the target audience. Again, this enables the marketer to build mutually-supportive relationships and a strong brand.
- *Clearly understanding the costs and benefits* to the customer from changing their behaviour. This concept, known as exchange analysis, springs from the social marketers' research and relationships. It means tailoring incentives and rewards and being aware of disincentives to change. Part of achieving change is the ability to identify and understand barriers and find effective ways of overcoming them. This level of insight and focus is provided by social marketing.

Businesses can also provide a powerful force for social and environmental change. However, this requires an organisation to build a value proposition that aligns with society's expectations and serves the common good. This proposition should create an implicit promise to society. In the future, it will be necessary for the commercial world not only to borrow increasingly from social marketing to build brand equity, but to embed social marketing and its principles fully into corporate strategy. Herein, there is a stern health warning to commercial marketers – beware false prophets, the eyes and ears of the world are upon you.

In the future, as well as expanding in the commercial sector, it seems likely that social marketing will continue to grow and develop in the place where it first came to prominence: in the public and not-for-profit sectors.

There are many policy issues where social marketing can help deliver real change. The serious issues we face in society today rely on fundamental changes in attitudes and behaviours; this is where social marketing can help to bring about necessary changes.

The position of social marketing is a privileged one, and the opportunity to make a difference and help create a better future is an incredibly worthwhile endeavour. It has already proven its worth in supporting campaigns to effect social and environmental change. But the challenges the world faces are immense and ever-changing; social marketing has a valuable role to play in helping to overcome these problems and improve the quality of life for everyone.

> Today, social marketing is increasingly relevant to the challenges of business and government: it will be indispensable in the future.

The chance for marketers to help the world tackle serious problems and make a real difference is inescapably exciting and unbelievably rewarding. With so much at stake, the question that we need to ask ourselves for the future is this: Is there more we can do? The answer: yes, always.

Key questions about social marketing

- Do you undertake rigorous scoping and research? For example, do you understand the barriers and motivation to change? What are the things that people need to move away from? What are the things that they need to move towards?
- Are you enabling people to change by providing them with relevant help and support?
- How will you ensure that people are actively involved and on board? How will you get people to become engaged and take responsibility for their actions?
- Are your communications two way and are you actively pursuing the idea of *co-production*?

continued on next page ...

- How well do you encourage people to change? Is it preferable to reward the new, desired behaviour or punish the old behaviour?
- Do you exemplify the approach and lead by example?
- Is piloting a technique used in your campaigns?
- When implementing a campaign, do you ask:
  - What capabilities do we have, and what skills and experience do we need to fill the gaps?
  - What is the schedule of activities and tasks, what do we have to deliver and when?
  - What resources do we need in order to meet the deadlines?
  - Who will be responsible for the different activities, and what will they need in order to achieve their tasks?
  - What systems, standards and procedures will we need for project management, managing data, monitoring progress, recording and reporting (to time and budget)?
  - What budget do we have and what contingencies do we have in place?
  - What are our requirements for commissioning and tendering to deliver and monitor our implementation plan?
  - What could go wrong, and how can we overcome possible difficulties?
- Does the focus on behaviour recognize what the individual needs to give up in order to receive the proposed benefits?
- Is there a clear understanding of what is competing for the audience's time and attention?
- Is your approach segmented, avoiding blanket approaches?
- Finally, are you using a mix of marketing methods?

Reference

CIM (2009) Less smoke, more fire: The benefits and impact of social marketing, *Shape the Agenda*, 15, Chartered Institute of Marketing.

INDEX